Hotel Grønland

Human use of caves and rock shelters in West Greenland

Clemens Pasda

BAR International Series 1309
2004

Published in 2016 by
BAR Publishing, Oxford

BAR International Series 1309

Hotel Grønland

ISBN 9781841716589 paperback
ISBN 9781407327341 e-format
DOI https://doi.org/10.30861/9781841716589
A catalogue record for this book is available from the British Library

BAR Publishing is the trading name of British Archaeological Reports (Oxford) Ltd.
British Archaeological Reports was first incorporated in 1974 to publish the BAR
Series, International and British. In 1992 Hadrian Books Ltd became part of the BAR
group. This volume was originally published by Archaeopress in conjunction with
British Archaeological Reports (Oxford) Ltd / Hadrian Books Ltd, the Series principal
publisher, in 2004. This present volume is published by BAR Publishing, 2016.

BAR
PUBLISHING

BAR titles are available from:

BAR Publishing
122 Banbury Rd, Oxford, OX2 7BP, UK
EMAIL   info@barpublishing.com
PHONE   +44 (0)1865 310431
FAX   +44 (0)1865 316916
www.barpublishing.com

Some years ago a young Dane accompanied Greenlandic hunters on a caribou-hunt south of Paamiut. Leaving their boat at the end of the fjord they started to approach the inland tundra by foot. After several hours of walking the Dane asked: "And where do we spend the night?" One of the hunters answered "Hotel Grønland!", which left the Dane wondering which kind of hotel one can expect in this hilly landscape. After some hours the group arrived at a rock shelter with caribou skins lying on the floor protected by the overhang. The hunter pointed at it and smiled: "Hotel Grønland!"

Story submitted by Klaus G. Hansen (Sisimiut 7/25/2000).

Contents

List of Figure 3

List of Tables 6

Acknowledgements 7

1. Introduction 9

2. Caves, rock shelters and boulders as part of the landscape 15

3. Naturally confined localities in West Greenland 23

    3.1 Variability in the use of caves, rock shelters and boulders 23

    3.2 Material record of occupation in rock shelters in the research area 40

4. Conclusions 75

Bibliography 77

List of figures

(if not annotated otherwise: all photos und drawings by the author)

Fig. 1: Research areas in 1999/2000 (1) and 2001/2002 (2) in the inland of Central West Greenland (map from Scholz 1991, fig. 1). 11

Fig. 2: Archaeological structures in West Greenland (from Gulløv 1983): 1 hut; 2-9 different types of massive houses; 10-12 tents; 13 rock shelter/cave; 14, 15 grave; 16 repository; 17 fox trap; 18 hopping stone-row; 19-21 *inussuit*; 22 shooting-covert. 12

Fig. 3: Sites found in a part of Angujaartorfiup Nunaa in 2001/02 with direction of historic umiaq travel routes (arrows) and surveyed area (broken line).
(map made by I. Seeberger (Erlangen) according to field-notes by the author). 19

Fig. 4: Spatial behaviour and site use in the inland of Central West Greenland during caribou population maximum (above) and minimum (below)
(changed figure after Pind et al. 1991: fig. 6.4). 22

Fig. 5a: Landscape in the inland of West Greenland (research area 1). 24

Fig. 5b: Landscape in the inland of West Greenland (research area 2). 24

Fig. 6: Boulders (site 9 in Pasda 1999) with proximal tibia and epiphysis of caribou (1), animal den (2), vertebra of hare (3), dwarf shrub vegetation (4) and ammunition *AMA 61* (5). 25

Fig. 7: Shooting-covert (site B16 in Grønnow/Meldgaard/Nielsen (1983).
Illustration see Fig. 21. 25

Fig. 8: *Inussuk* on top of large boulder (site FM 66V2-IV-133). 26

Fig. 9: Repository (site D1 in Grønnow/Meldgaard/Nielsen 1983) with natural rock (white), closing-stones (vertical hatching), dwarf-shrub vegetation (oblique hatching), caribou dung (1), carpal, phalanx, rib fragment, several long-bone fragments of caribou (2), tibia fragment and distal femur of caribou (3), 4 complete caribou metacarpus (4), caribou rib-fragment (5), caribou cranium with sawed antlers and chewing-marks (6), aluminium-bucket (7) and saw-blade (8). 27

Fig. 10: Deposits (71-73) in hollows under large boulders (sites 70-74 in Pasda 2000). 28

Fig. 11: Meat cache beside a natural boulder (site 31 in Pasda 1999). 29

Fig. 12: Small caribou hunting-drive system (sites 56-61 in Pasda 2000; no. 413 = site 413 in Pind et al.1991) with *inussuit* (58-61), shooting-covert (57), rock shelter (56), tent rings (413), equidistance 25m, lakes (hatched) and creeks (pointed). 29

Fig. 13: Archaeological structure (site 56 in Pasda 2000) with boulder (white), archaeological structure (grey), grass (hatched), edge of plateau (line with triangles), musk-ox wool (1), radius fragment of juvenile caribou (2). 30

Fig. 14a: *Inussuk* on historic route (site L323/L324 in Gabriel et al. 2002). 31

Fig. 14b: *Inussuk* on historic route (site L303 in Gabriel et al. 2002). 31

Fig. 15: Grave chamber under boulder (site L604 in Odgaard et al. 2003). 34

Fig. 16a: Remains of historic tent-house in front of south-facing rock wall
(site FM 66V2-II-015). 36

Fig. 16b: Remains of a Thule tent-house (site FM 66V2-II-031). 37

Fig. 17: Historic summer camp with tent-houses and deposits (site 24 in Pasda 1999), boulders
(white), turf wall (black), dwarf-shrub vegetation (hatched), edge of plateau (line with triangles). 37

Fig. 18: Tent-house (site 64 in Pasda 2000) built onto two natural boulders (white) with turf-wall
(black), indistinct turf wall (grey), dwarf-shrub vegetation (hatched) and edge of plateau (line
with triangles). 38

Fig. 19: Boulder with rectangular structure made out of stone (site 80 in Pasda 2000) with musk-
ox wool (1), boulder (white), drip line (broken line), archaeological structure (horizontal
hatched), grass vegetation (oblique hatched), edge of plateau (line with triangles). 42

Fig. 20: Boulder with two upright standing stones (site 62 in Pasda 2000) and caribou phalanx
(1), fine sediment (2), boulder (white), drip line (broken line) and archaeological structure
(hatched). 43

Fig. 21a: Resting and sleeping place in rock shelter (site FM 66V2-II-020) from west......................44

Fig. 21b: Resting and sleeping place in rock shelter (site FM 66V2-II-020) with musk-ox wool
(1), rock wall (hatched), drip line (broken line), archaeological structure (grey) and natural stones
(white)..45

Fig. 22: Resting and sleeping place in rock shelter (site FM 66V2-II-034) with natural hollow in
rock ceiling (1), rock wall (hatched), drip line (broken line), natural stones (white) and
archaeological structure made out of stone (grey) and turf (black). 46

Fig. 23a: Resting and sleeping place in rock shelter (site FM 66V2-II-025).
Illustration see fig. 22. 46

Fig. 23b: Resting and sleeping place in rock shelter (site FM 66V2-II-025) from east. 47

Fig. 24a: Rock wall with resting and sleeping places (site L609 in Odgaard et al. 2003) with
sketch of topographical situation (above), lake (grey), rock wall (hatched), boulder (white),
hunter's bed (1), used rock shelter (3). Illustration see fig. 22. 48

Fig. 24b: Rock wall with resting and sleeping places (site L609 in Odgaard et al. 2003) from east.....49

Fig. 24c: Hunters' bed 1 (site L609 in Odgaard et al. 2003) from east. 49

Fig. 24d: Used rock shelter 3 (site L609 in Odgaard et al. 2003) from southwest. 49

Fig. 25a: Rock wall with five resting and sleeping places (site FM 66V2-I-031) and sketch of
topographical situation (above), used rock shelter (1), hunters' beds (2-5).
Illustration see fig. 21 and 22. 50

Fig. 25b: Rock wall with five resting and sleeping places (site FM 66V2-I-031) from southwest.......51

Fig. 25c: Used rock shelter 1 (site FM 66V2-I-031) from northwest.......................................51

Fig. 25d: Hunters' bed 5 (site FM 66V2-I-031) from southwest..51

Fig. 26a: Resting and sleeping place in rock shelter (site L606 in Odgaard et al. 2003). Illustration see fig. 21 and 22. 52

Fig. 26b: Resting and sleeping place in rock shelter (site L606 in Odgaard et al. 2003) from north. 53

Fig. 26c: Resting and sleeping place in rock shelter (site L606 in Odgaard et al. 2003) from northwest. 53

Fig. 26d: Wall from resting and sleeping place in rock shelter (site 606 in Odgaard et al. 2003) from northwest. 54

Fig. 26e: Resting and sleeping place in rock shelter (site L606 in Odgaard et al. 2003) from southeast. 54

Fig. 27a: Boulder (site L620 in Odgaard et al. 2003) with resting and sleeping place (1), deposits (2-5), bone (6) and wooden arrow-shafts (7, 8). Illustration see Fig. 21 and 22. 56

Fig. 27b: Boulder (site L620 in Odgaard et al. 2003) with resting and sleeping place from east.......... 57

Fig. 27c: Boulder (site L620 in Odgaard et al. 2003) with deposit 4 from west. 57

Fig. 28a: Boulder (site FM 66V2-II-011) with natural shaled stone slab and archaeological structures from southeast. 58

Fig. 28b: Boulder (site FM 66V2-II-011) with tent-house-like structure from southeast. 58

Fig. 28c: Stone slab from boulder (site FM 66V2-II-011) with tent ring from northeast. 58

Fig. 28d: Boulder (site FM 66V2-II-011) with second tent-house-like structure from north................ 59

Fig. 28e: Boulder (site FM 66V2-II-011) with second tent-house-like structure from southeast.......... 59

Fig. 29a: Boulder (site FM 66V2-II-016) with resting and sleeping place (2), deposit (3), polarfox den (4), triangular structure (5), hunters' bed (6), shooting-coverts (7, 8), *inussuit* (9) and caribou pathes (grey). 61

Fig. 29b: Boulder (site FM 66V2-II-016) with resting and sleeping place 2 from northeast. 62

Fig. 30a: Resting and sleeping place in rock shelter (site L505 in Odgaard et al. 2003). Illustration see fig. 21. 62

Fig. 30b: Resting and sleeping place under boulder (site L505 in Odgaard et al. 2003) from south. ... 63

Fig. 30c: Inner part of resting and sleeping place under boulder (site L505 in Odgaard et al. 2003) from south. 63

Fig. 31: Single stones in row under drip line of rock shelter (site L531 in Odgaard et al. 2003).......... 64

Fig. 32a: Concentration of bones and antlers under east side of the overhanging boulder at the summer camp Qornoq kangigdleq (site L563 in Odgaard et al. 2003) from north............................... 65

Fig. 32b: Concentration of bones and antlers under north side of the overhanging boulder at the summer camp Qornoq kangigdleq (site L563 in Odgaard et al. 2003) from north............................... 66

Fig. 32c: Detail of the concentration of bones and antlers under north side of the overhanging boulder (site L563 in Odgaard et al. 2003) from north.. 66

Fig. 33a: Dubious archaeological structure in rock shelter (site FM 66V2-II-033).
Illustration see Fig. 21-23. 68

Fig. 33b: Dubious archaeological structure in rock shelter (site FM 66V2-II-033) from east. 69

Fig. 34a: Comparison of resting and sleeping places: used rock shelter (site FM 66V2-II-041). 71

Fig. 34b: Comparison of resting and sleeping places: hunters' bed
(site L557 in Odgaard et al. 2003). 72

Fig. 34c: Comparison of resting and sleeping places: hunters' bed
(site L560 in Odgaard et al. 2003). 72

List of tables

Tab. 1: Simplified model of site types and their occurrence in the inland of Central West Greenland (modified after Grønnow 1986 and Pind et al. 1991). 20

Tab. 2: Characteristics of used rock shelters in the inland of Central West Greenland......................... 71

Acknowledgements

This work is a product of ideas developed out of investigations of a number of Palaeolithic cave and rock shelter sites in South-West Germany, first in the 1980's as a student on excavations, later as the author's own research, but both as part of a research group led by the unforgotten Joachim *Kim* Hahn (1942-1997). A first enquiry about human use of caves in the Arctic was adressed in 1993 to Mikhail M. Bronshtein at Ekven in Chukotka. Pursuing this matter in 1998 led to field-work in Greenland from 1999-2002. The project started with scepticism about the usefulness of ethno-analogy (C. Pasda 1998) and has developed in directions nobody thought about before (K. Pasda 2001; in print; in prep.; C. Pasda 2001; 2002; 2003).

The following persons and institutions supported this research: The *Deutsche Forschungsgemeinschaft* (Bonn D) funded the whole project from 1999-2002. SILA / The Greenland Research Centre at the Danish National Museum invited us to take part and to incorporate our small-scale investigation in their project *"Habakuks hunting grounds"* from 2001-2002. The results presented in this book are based on sites seen, documented, discussed and on things learned during the field-work with SILA. Without this cooperation project our research would have been impossible. The project was situated from 1998-2003 at the *Institut für Ur- und Frühgeschichte* of the University Erlangen-Nuremberg. Ludwig Reisch, the head of that institute, as well as all members and students of that institute made us feel very much at home.

Joel Berglund (Greenland National Museum & Archives, Nuuk GL), Bjarne Grønnow and Hans Christian Gulløv (SILA/Danish National Museum, Copenhagen DK), Morten Meldgaard (North Atlantic Bridge, Copenhagen DK), Patrick Plumet (Université du Québec, Montreal CAN) and Douglas R. Stenton (Inuit Heritage Trust, Iqaluit CAN) were open-minded to all my questions before field-work started. Stan Meuffels (Karrimor Germany, Neuss D) was a great help by generously providing us with equipment. Martin Street (Forschungsbereich Altsteinzeit des Römisch-Germanischen Zentralmuseums, Neuwied D) made the main correction, Sven Feldmann (University Erlangen-Nuremberg D) the last correction of the English version of the manuscript (which was finished in March 2004) and are not responsible for my argumentation and mistakes.

Klaus G. Hansen and Nathan Larsen (both Sisimiut Museum, Sisimut GL) made us welcome in Sisimiut in 2000. Klaus had the idea to make the interviews with Geerteeraq Dahl (Itilleq), Laarseeraq Enoksen (Sarfannguaq), Seth Olesen (Ikerasaarsuk) and Ulrik Lennert (Sarfannguaq): *Qujanaq*! Bent Brodersen (Kangerlussuaq International Science Support, Kangerlussuaq GL) gave, always in high spirits, reliable support during all field-seasons. The families Krug, Bock (both Kassel D) and Pasda (Ludwigsburg D) made it possible for a family to do field-work.

In Habakuks hunting grounds it was an unforgettable pleasure to work and live together with Charlotte Damm (Tromsø University NOR), Mille Gabriel, Bjarne Grønnow, Ulla Odgaard (all SILA/Danish National Museum, Copenhagen DK). The summer of 2002, in particular, was the best time ever spent in Greenland! Bjarne Grønnow, director of SILA, was the greatest help throughout the whole project, from its initiation, during field-work and with comments on an earlier version of the manuscript. When I first visited him in Lejre in 1998 nobody could imagine that four years later – after following the Greenlanders' routes to the large summer camps at Tasersiaq – we would both spend his birthday on a rainy, *Mordor*-like boulder-field at 1100m a.s.l. consuming the last of the chocolate while burning a small candle: Thank you very much!

Last but not least: Thank you Kerstin, the best partner in the field - and, of course, in life.

Since, in the far inland of West Greenland, one can stay for weeks without encountering other people we were delighted in 2000 to meet two caribou-hunters and their sons. Of course they were citizens of modern Sisimiut but after trying to communicate, laughing a lot - while, as we had neither tea nor cigarettes, sharing muesli-bars with their sons - it was obvious that we as scientists do not belong there at all. After thinking further about it: We are here just to learn, to widen our horizons and to accept the limits of our scientific approaches. Therefore, after five consecutive Greenlandic summers I can now only say "*Nuanneqaaq!*", hoping that this work is seen with interest in Greenland today.

Therefore this book is dedicated to all Greenlanders in past and present who walked the routes inland which I had the privilege to follow.

Ludwigsburg, in February 2004

1. Introduction

The formation of caves and rock shelters depends on geological structures and geomorphological processes. Consequently their occurrence is tied to rock formations, e.g. bedrock, rock walls or boulders. Therefore caves and rock shelters are spatially fixed elements of a landscape which are present over a long time period. This definition – sites which are fixed in space and time - is emphasized by archaeologists (e.g. Straus 1997, 1; Walthall 1998, 224) and is more important for characterizing them than spelaeological definitions like space proportions or illumination by daylight (e.g. Trimmel 1968, 7). But then even barely overhanging rock walls or a single, small boulder also meet this definition, as can be seen from Palaeolithic and Mesolithic sites in Central Europe (e.g. Hahn 1984; Pousaz 1991, Fig. 4). As caves and rock shelters are spatially and temporally stable elements of a landscape they have certain characteristics which remain unchanged and therefore predicable over long time periods: This is the restricted space of these *"naturally confined locations"* (Galanidou 2000, 244), e.g. between rock wall and slope (Barton/Clark 1993, 47; Walthall 1998, 224), and their exposure to sun, wind, insects, cold and moisture or their distance from resources such as fuel, water and food (Straus 1979, 332-333).

No region provides as much information on human use of caves and rock shelters as Central and Western Europe. Here caves were already designated as dwelling places of the first humans by the philosophers of the classical antiquity (Schama 1995, 526; Stoczkowski 2002, 30-31), something which influenced prehistoric research when scientific investigations in a modern sense began some 100-150 years ago (Farrand 1985, 21; Hahn 1990). Since then hunter-gatherer archaeology has focused so much on caves that open-air sites are rarely known in some regions, e.g. Cantabria (Straus 1979, 332) or Southwest Germany (Eriksen 1991, 79). Caves and rock shelters in Central Europe are viewed today as repeatedly used sites but as representing only a small part of all the localities used by prehistoric humans (Straus 1997, 1). Nevertheless, it is not easy to prove the prehistoric use of caves in Central Europe as archaeological layers can be eroded or buried under meter-deep sediments (Grote 1990, 137; Straus 1990, 258-260).

Detailed archaeological excavations have shown that caves were used for different reasons by Palaeolithic humans: Dark and deep parts of caves far away from the entrance have been used as can be demonstrated by cave art (e.g. Lorblanchet 1999), foot prints (Clottes 1993; Garcia/Rouzaud 2001) or artefacts on the cave floor and on the walls (Begouën et al. 1996). This is interpreted as either real occupation and settlement (e.g. Begouën et al. 1989, 168-169; Utrilla/Mazo/Domingo 2003) or ritual activities in caves (e.g. Owens/Hayden 1997). Rock shelters and caves have been used in winter, sometimes in alternation with bears (Münzel 2002; Münzel/Morel/Hahn 1994, 76; Münzel et al. 2001, 324), as repositories for clothes, equipment or as protection against bad weather (Hahn 1986, 217; 1993, 240). This use over hundreds or thousands of years (Galanidou 2000, 272; Nicholson/Cane 1991, 263; Straus 1997), together with different natural and cultural processes (Bar-Yosef 1993, 16-19; Fernández-Jalvo/Andrews 2000; Straus 1993, 3-5) has led to archaeological layers in sometimes complex stratigraphies with both vertical and horizontal hiatuses (Farrand 1993; 2001).

New time-consuming and expensive excavations of Palaeolithic sites in Central Europe today provide a first opportunity to investigate the use of caves and rock shelters by Ice-Age humans. Analogies from recent and historic hunter-gatherers of other continents are problematical from a scientific as well as from an ethical point of view (e.g. David/Kramer 2001; 48-52, 227; Gosden 1999, 9; Kelly 1995, 333-344; Stahl 1993; Zvelebil/Fewster 2001). Among others, Galanidou (1998) and Spikins (2000) have recently pointed out the overly simplistic application of ethnographic evidence in modelling Palaeolithic and Mesolithic settlement patterns. Often models are built by taking processes and relations found in our so-called 'Western culture' as deriving from human nature (Gosden 1999, 165-166). That means that our 'Western culture' provides only limited experience and knowledge about humans with other ways of life (David/Kramer 2001, 1). Therefore an investigation in a region where hunter-gatherers used caves and rock shelters in historic or recent times gives an opportunity to expand our knowledge about people which lived at other times and in other parts of the world (Bernbeck 1997,

108). Investigations of recent cave use show us reasons for occupation and for the appearance, size and number of structures (Galanidou 1997, 23), examples of the management of restricted space by individuals and groups (Gamble 1991, 10-11), and allow recognition of natural characteristics of caves and rock shelters (Balme/Beck 2002, 157; Theunissen/Balme/Beck 1998) as well as general trends and the place of caves and rock shelters in a large-scale settlement pattern (Galanidou 2000, 273). This is not simply uncritical analogy (see Kötter 2001), since this research can explain how an archaeological context is produced by a living culture, which are the factors responsible for that transformation and which comparisons between cultures are possible (David/Kramer 2001, 101). Therefore the research presented here "*does not aim at explanation at any price. Its main ambition is to establish an empirical testable correspondance between the world and the hypothesis we form from it*" (Stoczkowski 2002, 179). On the other hand this kind of research brings the critical recognition that our own traditions, positions and convictions impose upon us a subjective scientific perspective (e.g. Clifford 1988; Geertz 1988). This has various implications for our view of other cultures (Gosden 2001) and of our own culture (Clifford/Marcus 1986; Marcus/Fischer 1986, 137-138), a phenomenon referred to as a "*Western Gaze*" (Bender 1999, 31). Therefore a scientist has to be aware "*that all research and writing, including one's own, has sociopolitical content and implication [...and...] results not only from the scientific paradigm to which we adhere, but also from our political and social perspectives*" (David/Kramer 2001, 55) or from our myths (Schama 1995, 134, 574). Seen at a larger scale (Daniel 2002, 15, 91, 388, 400) a scientific result is just formulated knowledge which is generally accepted by others at a certain time. This knowledge should be an outcome of the reflection of subjective attitudes of the scientists as it is relational and objectified by defined scientific methods and theoretical background. Whereas a scientific result is not necessarily better or more objective than non-scientific explanations, a scientific explanation should be right, useful and justified, something for which the scientist takes responsibility.

The conference "The human use of caves" (Bonsall/Tolan-Smith 1997) and a recent investigation of published reports (Galanidou 2000; additional: Binford 1996; Moser 1999) show that research on the use of caves and rock shelters by recent and historic hunter-gatherers is far from exhaustive. In addition, research on the use of caves in Neolithic times follows other scientific goals (e.g. Brochier et al. 1992; Perrin/Sordoillet/Voruz 2002). The published reports show that research on hunter-gatherer cave use is restricted to tropical and desert-like environments of the southern hemisphere and is focused on ethno-archaeological and ethno-historic studies as well as on investigations of sites abandoned recently. Recent research on caves in arctic environments is mainly focused on the taphonomy of animal remains (e.g. Cinq-Mars 1979; Georgina 2001; Sattler 1997; Sattler/Vinson/Gillispie 2001) with only brief statements published about cave use by northern hunter-gatherers: e.g. overnight stays in rock shelters and caves were mentioned from the 18th century (Hearne 1981, 145-146, 151) until today (Binford 1978, 489-491; Lauriol et al. 2001, 138; Larsen 1968, 11-12). Against this background the Institute of Prehistory at the University of Erlangen-Nuremberg (Germany) conducted between 1999 and 2002 the project "*The use of caves and rock shelters in West Greenland*". Both in August of 1999 and 2000 two persons conducted a four week survey (C. Pasda 2001; 2002; 2003; K. Pasda 2001; in print). In 2001 and 2002 this research was incorporated in the project "*Habakuks hunting grounds – Coast-, fjord and inland dwellers: prehistoric and historic settlement patterns in Central West Greenland*" led by SILA / The Greenland Research Centre at the Danish National Museum in Copenhagen. Field-work was carried out during three and four weeks in July and August by four to five archaeologists (Gabriel et al. 2002; Odgaard et al. 2003).

It was obvious that human cave use can only be understood in the context of the entire settlement and subsistence pattern of the investigated region (Gamble 1991, 11). Therefore the inland of the Sisimiut Municipality in Central West Greenland (Fig. 1: 1) was chosen as the research area. According to Møbjerg (1998, 99) this region is the best investigated area in Greenland concerning resource description, settlement structure and social organization. Kapel (1996, 120) and Schilling (1996, 117) annotate that this area is the most extensively archaeologically surveyed inland area in Greenland. Historic sources date as far back as 300 years (Møbjerg 1998): Missionaries, later expeditions and colonial managers made notes about social and settlement structure, material culture and the use of resources. The settlement pattern of historic Greenlanders is described in detail by different archaeological, ethno-historic and archaeozoological investigations (chapter 2). By contrast, the area in Angujaartorfiup Nunaa in the Maniitsoq Municipality which was investigated in 2001 and 2002 (Fig. 1: 2) was a more or less unknown territory from an archaeological point of view. Here only regions more close to the Kangerlussuaq fjord and in the *Paradise Valley* have seen extensive field-work (Grønnow 1986; Kapel 1996; Secher et al. 1987) which is supported by detailed ethno-historic sources (e.g. Lidegaard 1986; Thisted 1997; 1999).

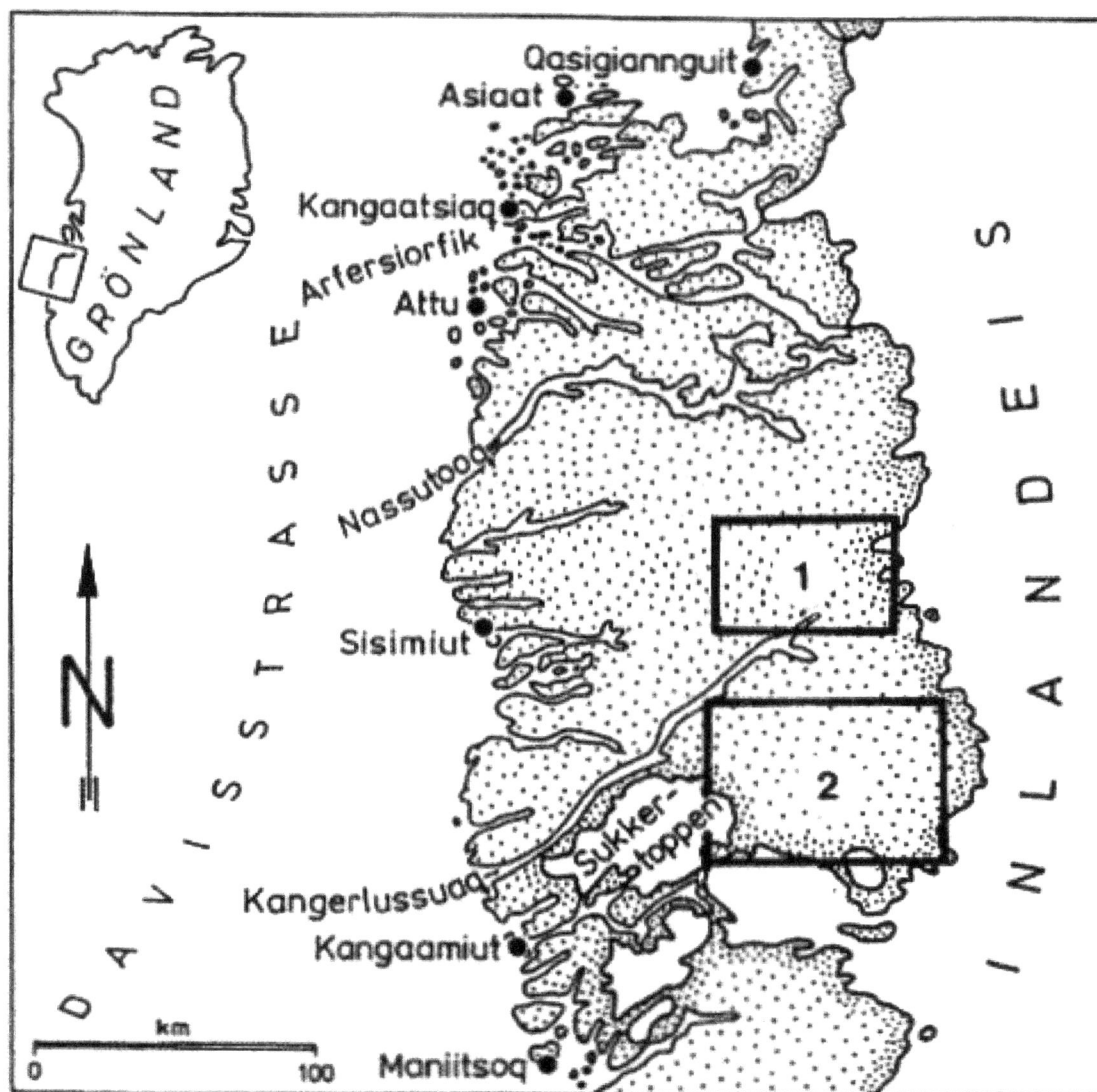

Fig. 1: Research areas in 1999/2000 (1) and 2001/2002 (2) in the inland of Central West Greenland (map from Scholz 1991, fig. 1).

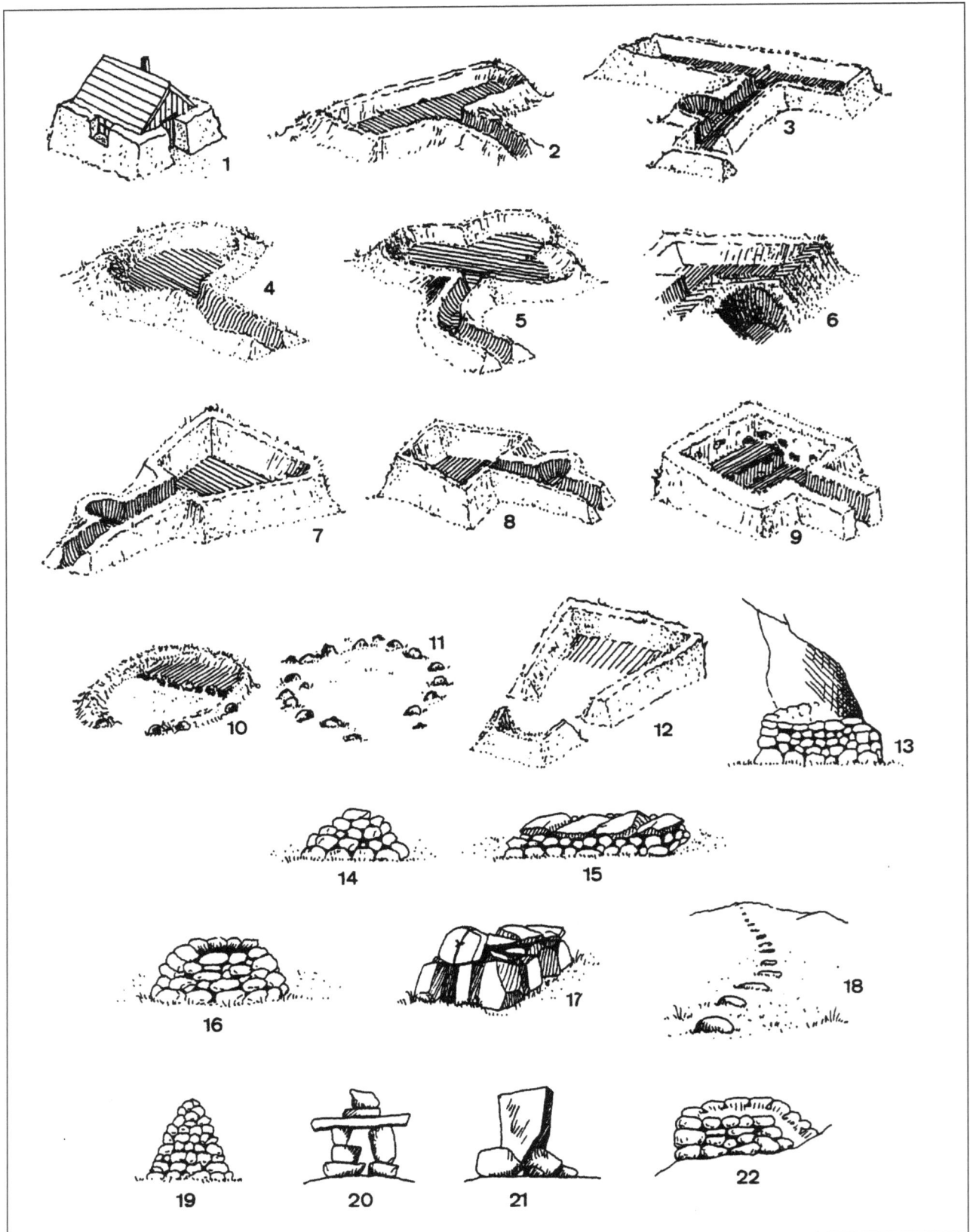

Fig. 2: Archaeological structures in West Greenland (from Gulløv 1983): 1 hut; 2-9 different types of massive houses; 10-12 tents; 13 rock shelter/cave; 14, 15 grave; 16 repository; 17 fox trap; 18 hopping stone-row; 19-21 inussuit; 22 shooting-covert.

The use of caves during caribou-hunting is mentioned for both regions in historic times (e.g. Rink 1875, 463; 1877, 232-241; Thisted 1999, 394, 460). Of course in West Greenland modern caribou-hunting differs from subsistence foraging of the last three centuries (see Dahl 2000, 160-168) and the use of new material changed the kind of cave-use, e.g. the use of canvas tents made hunters more independent of caves (R. Petersen 2003, 42). Nevertheless, caves and rock shelters have also been used during hunting in modern times (oral information K.G. Hansen, Sisimiut 7/25/2000): Here the used caves and rock shelters are designated as *Hotel Grønland*, to show the Europeans in an ironic way but with pride: *"See, this is how we lived out here long before you came around"* (e-mail K. G. Hansen, Sisimiut 2/8/2003). This can be seen in Greenland and north-eastern Canada where rock walls and large boulders were incorporated in the construction of houses, tents, fireplaces or caches since Palaeo-Eskimo times (e.g. Jensen 1996, 150-151; Knuth 1981, 94; Schledermann 1990, 98-99, 295-296).

An additional advantage of choosing the inland of West Greenland as research area is its highly visible archaeological record and that a huge amount of data can be obtained by field-surveys alone (Fig. 2). Therefore the research in Greenland was no classical ethno-archaeological study, with the observation of human behaviour and documentation of its archaeological consequences (O'Connell 1995, 206). Field-work in Greenland was based on searching for and documenting archaeological structures of prehistoric, historic and recent sites. Typology, function and use of structures and sites were known from written sources as well as from previous archaeological work, mentioned in detail in chapter 2. Since David/Kramer (2001, 2-13) incorporate different research strategies and studies into the term ethno-archaeology, the present investigation can be seen as falling into their broader definition too.

The rock outcrops in the research areas are mainly basement gneisses and granites, with locally interstratified and folded belts of metasediments and metavolcanics (Escher/Sørensen/Zeck 1976). Frost is an important factor of shaping the landscape (Hansen 1970, 31-35) as it disintegrates, exfoliates and shatters rock into angular blocks of different size. Rockfall produces scree slopes with fine fragments near the top and large blocks (several meters in diameter) near the base (Everett 1967, 26). Due to the domination of gneisses landslides are rare (Pedersen et al. 2002). Due to long submergence by glacier ice and slight tectonic raising the Sisimiut inland between the upper Kangerlussuaq and the Isortoq (Fig. 1: 1) has only rounded hills up to 500m a.s.l. transected by several west / east oriented valleys with creeks and lakes. Angujaartorfiup Nunaa in the Maniitsoq Municipality (Fig. 1: 2) has a comparable morphology only in its northern part and near the upper part of the Kangerlussuaq Fjord, whereas the entire remaining region is defined by northwest / southeast oriented valleys with lakes, creeks and rivers flowing in north-western and western direction (Fig. 3). These valleys are accompanied by mountains and plateaus of 1000-1500m a.s.l. Lakes are characteristic for the landscape: Anderson et al. (2002) estimate there are approximately 20,000 lakes in the research areas. Dwarf shrubland with mainly willow and some other species occurs to about 250m a.s.l. only (Bøcher 1963, 161) and is accompanied, among other vegetation types, by dry grass communities, herb mats and fresh water communities. Areas above 700m a.s.l. contain minimal vegetation and may be of little importance as caribou food sources (Cuyler et al. 2002, 17). Regionally, West Greenland has experienced a decline in average temperature in the second half of the 20th century (Brodersen/Lindegaard/Anderson 2001, 59; Mayer et al. 2002, 154). Typical for West Greenland are decadal periods with changes in temperatures (Mayer et al. 2002, 154; Willemse 2000, 145). The inland climate (Bøcher 1949; Rott/Obleitner 1992; Willemse 2000, 48-49) is of a continental type (mean annual temperature: -5°C) with a cold winter (approximately mean in February: -26°C) followed by a warm and dry summer (approximately mean in July: +11°C). Annual precipitation is low (<200mm) and occurs mainly in summer, but in summer evaporation exceeds precipitation at an annual scale which leads closed basin lakes to become saline (Anderson et al. 2002, 145). At ground level easterly winds dominate near the inland ice (Willemse 2000).

During the 15 weeks of field-work every site was documented by a measured plan, a written description and photograph. The ground-plan was measured by either one or two persons with tape-measure and metre rule. Cross-sections were made in the same manner but in a smaller scale. Due to bad weather or time lack some sites could not be measured that exactly (Fig. 10; 27). At two sites overview sketches of the topographical situation were made (Fig. 24; 25). Due to technical problems in August 2000 it was impossible to document some sites (Fig. 10, 18-20) photographically. Location was taken by hand-held

GPS but is not presented here. Field-work was further supported by interviews conducted by Nathan Larsen in 2001 with Geerteeraq Dahl from Itilleq, Laarseeraq "Assa" Enoksen and Ulrik Lennert from Sarfannguaq and Seth Olesen from Ikerasaarsuk which were translated into English by Klaus G. Hansen (Hansen/Larsen 2002). In the Arctic exact dating of sites visible on the surface is difficult without the help of the natural sciences (Kramer 1996, 39). Approximate and relative dating is possible using the rare artefacts around or inside structures (e.g. Grønnow/Meldgaard/Nielsen 1983, 27, 30-31, 53, 65-68) or the form of the structures and their state of preservation as well as the degree of lichen cover of structures (e.g. Grønnow 1986, 72; Pind et al. 1991, 59-68; Secher et al. 1987, 58). Identification of site type and explanation of site function are possible using historic and ethno-historic sources (e.g. Gulløv 1983). In Greenland this method was applied with success (see Gulløv 1997, 26-29) and has a good potential for interpretation of both single structures (e.g. Møbjerg/Caning 1986; Møbjerg/Robert-Lamblin 1989) and entire regions (e.g. Grønnow/Meldgaard/Nielsen 1983; Gulløv 1997; Sandell/Sandell 1991).

2. Caves, rock shelters and boulders as part of the landscape

In Germany the term *Kulturlandschaft* is defined by geographers (e.g. Leser 1997, 277) as a natural environment altered in different ways by human culture. That infers that nature and culture are separated parts of the world, which has implications for scientific research in so called *Landschaftsarchäologie* (e.g. Lüning 1997; Schade 2000) where the natural sciences and humanities have clearly divided approaches for investigating the changing relationship between culture and environment over a longer time span. Even Palaeolithic archaeologists have used this definition twenty years ago (e.g. Müller-Beck 1983, 14; 1986, 44), which might seem to imply that hunter-gatherers are only influenced by the environment and have no cultural relationship to the landscape. However, the landscape is not just a part of nature seen from the outside by a cultural being – this being a 'western' view of the world, possibly not older than 500 years (see discussion in Layton/Ucko 1999, 3). Landscapes are cultural before they are natural, representing constructs of our imagination (Schama 1995, 31). Landscape is not merely the world we see but a construction and composition of that world, therefore representing a way of seeing the world (Cosgrove 1984, 13). Humans live and move in a landscape, they change it and have a relationship to a landscape in the way that they perceive landscape and environment, its material culture and architecture, its changes and its history. A landscape is thus an entity that exists by virtue of its beings, perceived, experienced and contextualized by people (Knapp/Ashmore 1999, 1). Landscape is indeed created by people through their engagement with the world around them (Bender 1993, 1). Therefore the landscape is not an abstract natural space with investigable objective characteristics independent of human culture. In contrast landscape is experienced and valued by humans through action and material culture (e.g. Gosden 1999, 153-154, 158-159). Landscape is also an expression for the process by which all people understand and engage with the material world around them (Bender 2001, 3) as a contextual horizon of perceptions in which people act and feel themselves to be living in their world (Stewart/Strathern 2003, 4). This "*humanised (...) landscape*" (Muir 1999, 75) is an assemblage of quantitative and qualitative aspects of components present which reflect the different uses applied to the natural surface. The idea of a social landscape (Gosden/Head 1994, 113-114) reverses the concept of environmental determinism and treats the environment as a space in which human skills are deployed and where material settings are not external to social being, but constructed through past human action. *Landscape archaeology* tries to (re-)unify nature and culture and to take into consideration cognitive systems and expressions of meaning (Layton/Ucko 1999, 12) and of chronologies of places from their creation and use until today (Barrett 1999, 25-26). Thomas (2001, 165-166) emphasized that within this thematic discussion of landscape archaeologists have been most willing to question some of the received norms of the discipline: Period, sequence, identity, objectivity, and writing about the past.

A general discussion of the perception of the environment by hunter-gatherers was represented by Ingold (2000): Hunter-gatherers do not perceive landscape as land, nature, space or a function useful for exploitation. Neither is landscape a neutral part of nature in contrast to human behaviour. Hunter-gatherers see neither our 'western' contrast between civilization and wilderness nor a cultural sphere in contrast to nature (Klein 1994). Through travelling and dwelling hunter-gatherers are not spectators from outside but actors and participants in the landscape and a part of it. For hunter-gatherers landscape is created by a large record of both active experience and of their ancestors who dwelled in the landscape and left objects, stories and myths, and who created and used certain localities. Landscape is created and formed by events in the past and actual interaction of humans and non-humans, animated and unanimated beings and their ongoing relationship. Therefore landscape is a qualitative perceived and heterogeneous world. For the Arctic, the perception of the landscape by hunter-gatherers is described among others by Anawak (1989), Bielawski (1989) or Doubleday (1999), for West Greenland in pre-colonial/historic times e.g. by Birket-Smith (1924, 430-459). Always connected with foraging waysof life is short- or long-distance mobility and hence orientation possibilities (for the Arctic among others: Bielawski 1989, 230; Burch 1975; Fortescue 1988; Gulløv 1997, 400; H.C. Petersen 1986a, 262; 1986b, 161-189; R. Petersen 1973; Robbe 1977; Rowley 1985). Travelling, dwelling and activities, individual experiences, stories, myths and legends, learning and apprenticeship (e.g. Nuttall 2000), teaching, information exchange and social interaction all lead to detailed knowledge about resources and their spatial and temporal occurrence. This *"landscape learning process"* (Rockman 2003, 12) is a basic presupposition of foraging lifeways (e.g. Kelly 1995, 97-98, 150-151). This knowledge can be seen in names for landscapes, rivers, camps, fords etc. (H.C. Petersen 1986a, 262; Gripp 1941/42, 41), legends and stories connected with promontories and creeks (Birket-Smith 1924, 219) or interviews concerning *"traditional ecological knowledge"* (e.g. Cruikshank 2001; Ferguson/Messier 1997; Ferguson/Williamson/Messier 1998; Usher 2000). Place names do not just name localities, they characterize certain physical, biological, ecological, sacral or mythical attributes, they create pathways (Zedeño/Stoffle 2003, 61-65), connect places with stories from the past and make orientation and path-finding in a landscape possible (Ingold 2000, 219, 232; Golledge 2003, 36; Kelly 2003, 45-47; MacDonald 1998, 162, 188-191). Localities are also connected with individuals, families or groups: In Greenland it was not the territories around hunting camps themselves but specific identifiable points in a landscape, like net sites, mooring facilities, hunters' houses, tent rings, smoking chambers etc., which were connected with rights of ownership as the residents family's first claim (R. Petersen 2003, 60). Here a territory may be owned by individual families, but that does not exclude others from hunting or fishing in this area (Dahl 2000, 171-173). The knowledge about landscape can also be seen in detailed maps made by Inuit (e.g. Bender 1999, 40; Gulløv 2000; Hallendy 1994, fig. 3; Holm 1914, 107-108; Mathiassen 1928, 97-100; Secher et al. 1987, 64-65; Spink/Moodie 1972; Thalbitzer 1914, 665-666) which are known from the research area too (Thisted 1997, 228-229; 1999, 535-537): Here a map made by the Greenlander Jens Kreutzmann in 1863 shows valleys, plateaux, travel routes and camp sites with nearly 300 place names. This map was the basis of field-survey conducted in research area 2. As forms of map use have been an integral part of recorded human history (Golledge 2003, 40) one can imagine that arctic hunter-gatherers were familiar with all geological phenomena such as places to obtain minerals (Hansen et al. 1978, 60; H.C. Petersen 1986b, 17) and the locations of boulders, boulder groups, erratic blocks and caves too (Gripp 1941/42, 40-41).

These more general statements can be verified for the research area by ethno-historic sources and archaeological evidence: The story of a couple from Qerrortusoq near Sisimiut which hunted caribou in summer 1866 (Rink 1877, 232-241) shows that they followed a sort of 'mental' (see Muir 1999, 126-127) or 'cognitive map' (Golledge 2003, 303). For example, they knew where the best protected rock shelter was situated during bad weather: *"We went to look for a place of shelter, because the rain was pouring down faster and faster, but the only cave that I knew of to be fit for sleeping in was still four miles off (...)"* (Rink 1877, 233). The same is told by Geerteeraq Dahl: *"When you go on overnight trips around Itilleq there are no caves that are good enough to use. But if you were to look up Qoororsuaq it has lots of boulders where it should be possible to find shelter possibilities due to many boulders that have fallen down from the mountain (...)"* (Hansen/Larsen 2002). Not only the geographical position but the general meaning and the main function of caves are known: *"(...) at noon we reached a cave below a large fragment of rock, which the boat-parties from Kangerdlugsuak use for their sleeping-place. In this place we rested and had a meal"* (Rink 1877, 238). As caves and rock shelters were well known they had names which is, as mentioned above, important for path-finding and orientation. Laarseeraq "Assa" Enoksen from Sarfannguaq related: *"I only know about one cave called the Wolf's Cave (amaqqat inaat). It was once the home for wolves. My grand-father once pointed it out for me. It is located near the Taseqqap saqqaa"* (Hansen/Larsen 2002). One has to remember that this cave is named for an animal which does not, or only very rarely, occurs in Central West Greenland (Dawes/Elander/Ericson 1986). Tobias Mouritzen, born in 1892, mentioned the name Napassoq for a boulder which was used regularly for overnight stays and as a cache while travelling for several days from the summer camp Eqalummiut to the large lake Tasersiaq and back (Grønnow 1986, 78). Another named boulder in research area 2 is documented in a watercolour from the 19th century (Thisted 1999, 507). Geerteeraq Dahl told about a boulder west of the research area which was used in a similar manner: *"After having walked Qoororsuaq going east towards the end of the valley near the turn, we got to Tunuliarfik. It is a plain area with a huge boulder called Sinittarfissuaq. Depending on which way you approach the boulder you can see small piles of rocks on either side of the boulder. This is where we go for overnight shelter"* (Hansen/Larsen 2002). Sometimes caves were very small and could be used by only a few individuals. Using such localities with a large group made organization in advance necessary, e.g. by carrying a tent. Geerteeraq Dahl told about this situation: *"West of the lake is a small steep hill not far from the stream, where there is a small cave with space for three people (...).*

(...) it is made out of rocks, it is not very big, the end of it is closed up and it also has a very low ceiling making entry hard. We have to crawl in, almost lying down. When we are many people we sat up a tent in front of it. The cave is nice and dry to sleep in it. (...) a small fireplace is to be found" (Hansen/Larsen 2002). Of course areas without caves and rock shelters were known. Staying in these areas involved other strategies, as told by Geerteeraq Dahl: *"There are no shelters or storage places to leave things. (...) People used tents all the time"* (Hansen/Larsen 2002). And Laarseeraq "Assa" Enoksen: *"There are not many storage places around Sarfannguaq, therefore we make sure to collect lots of firewood and we sleep beneath cliffs(...). Because there are not many caves in the inland, we make sure to camp where there is plenty of vegetation. We keep warm with each others body heat"* (Hansen/Larsen 2002).

Detailed information about the use of the inland by Greenlanders is published in different historic, ethno-historic and archaeological sources (e.g. Bøcher et al. 1980, 60-65; Grønnow 1986; Grønnow/Meldgaard/Nielsen 1983; M. Meldgaard 1983; H.C. Petersen 1986a; 1986b, 165-171; Pind et al. 1991; Secher et al. 1987, 52-72). Several stable or continuous elements of inland landscape use can be shown: In West Greenland the annual economic cycle (Grønnow/ Meldgaard/Nielsen 1983, 21-22; Kleivan 1984, 522; M. Meldgaard 1983, 263) was dominated in historic times by subsistence on sea animals like seals, whales or fish. Therefore Greenlanders lived almost the whole year at different winter settlements on the coast or in the fjords. An exception existed in Central West Greenland where the inland region of the municipalities of Aasiat, Sisimiut and Maniitsoq (Fig. 1) was used in summer and autumn to hunt caribou. The journey inland from winter settlements started in summer (Grønnow/Meldgaard/Nielsen 1983, Fig. 14, 70-72) using umiaqs to transport people and equipment by boat from the coast via fjords to the larger lakes or rivers, sometimes by carrying everything overland. At certain places umiaqs and seafaring equipment were cached and the journey inland continued by foot. This walk inland lasted some days during which the group stayed at certain places or localities to rest or spend the night using tents (Fig. 2: 10, 11), rock shelters (Fig. 2: 13) or just by staying in the open. Sometimes kayaks were carried along too (R. Petersen 2003, 39, 44) or small vessels were built with tent poles and skins (Birket-Smith 1924, 257-258).

Caribou-hunting inland was carried out in two main ways. In the first, a small group or a number of hunters stalked caribou over a large area for a longer period, staying for only short time at several localities (Fig. 2: 2-13) and sometimes walking approximately 175km a week (H.C. Petersen 1986a, 265). In the second, a larger summer camp with many massive houses (Fig. 2: 2-9) was used for the whole hunting-season by a larger group or some families. When possible, fishing was involved too (Grønnow 1986, 72). Those summer camps are often situated in topographical places resembling a bottleneck situation where caribou were forced to come to certain areas which are useful for hunting deer. Often this bottleneck situation was strengthened by artificial hunting-drive systems (Grønnow/Meldgaard/Nielsen 1983; R. Petersen 2003, 210) with single cairns (Fig. 2: 19-21), stone-rows and fences (Rosing 1988), shooting-coverts (Fig. 2: 22) and meat-caches (Fig. 2: 16). The summer camps were also important cultural centers, as information was exchanged, disputes were discussed or new partners were found (Grønnow/Meldgaard/Nielsen 1983, 37; M. Meldgaard 1983, 265; R. Petersen 2003, 96-97). In the hinterland of the summer camps can be found smaller camps, single tent rings (Fig. 2: 11), small-scale hunting-drives, overnight camps (Fig. 2: 10, 11, 13) and specialized sites (Fig. 2: 17, 22) which were used by small groups to stay for one night during special hunting expeditions, transport or processing. At the end of the hunting season the same routes and strategies were used to bring the obtained game back to the winter settlements. Single persons, families and groups met on their way to the inland region and back, e.g. at the places where the umiaqs had been left, or at the mouths of secondary valleys leading to large fjords. Here were located short-time aggregation sites, e.g. Angujaartorfik at the southern coast of the upper Kangerlussaq (Kapel 1996, 121), where social contacts and information exchange between the different groups occurred (H.C. Petersen 1986b, 168-169).

Another typical site type in Central West Greenland is the *hunters' bed* (Grønnow 1986, 72; Grønnow/Meldgaard/Nielsen 1983, 52; Pind et al. 1991, 59-60; Secher et al. 1987, 58): This is a square, or sometimes rounded structure, measuring from 1x1,5m to 2x2, and up to 4x2m, and with up to 50cm high walls built of stone and turf (Fig. 24a: 1; 24c; 25a: 4, 5; 15d; 29a: 6; 34: b, c; Pasda 2003; Abb. 1-6). Sometimes large natural boulders and rock walls are incorporated as part of the wall (e.g. Holtved 1944, 28-29; Johnson 1933, 54; Pasda 2003, Abb. 5). The hunters' bed was filled with twigs, heather or skin and was used without a roof in order to spend the night during caribou-hunts. Pictures from the 19th century (e.g. Rink 1877, 104) show typical domestic activities like cooking, processing of meat and skin, maintenance of weapons around a hunters' bed during a caribou-hunting expedition. This structure was used over centuries (Grønnow/Meldgaard/Nielsen 1983, 53).

In the research area this form of inland occupation by Neo-Eskimos persisted during at least 700 years (chapter 3.2). In contrast, the nature of inland occupation in Central West Greenland by Palaeo-Eskimos remains obscure (see discussion by Schilling 1996), even though unquestionable Palaeo-Eskimo tent rings were found in 2001 and 2002 by B. Grønnow in the inner region of research area 2 (Gabriel et al. 2002; Odgaard et al. 2003): These structures can be compared with sites at the upper fjord (Kapel 1996) and are dated with one ^{14}C sample to between 1800-1600 BC.

The continuous elements in the use of the inland region by Neo-Eskimos mentioned above have resulted in site types of characteristic appearance (Fig. 2) which occur in a typical pattern in the landscape (Grønnow 1986, 78; Kapel 1996, 127-128; Pind et al. 1991, 52-57): Assembly camps occur at the fjords where family groups met before and after their inland journeys (Tab. 1). Larger camps are situated at the end of umiaq routes along lakes and rivers where seafaring equipment was left. Small sites, in the form of single tent rings, rock shelters and hunters' beds represent sleeping and resting places along the route inland. Most large camps are situated in the centre of the main caribou-hunting area. Small sites used to rest or to spend the night are located in the hinterland of those main camps and were used by special hunting groups and possibly by carriers during hunting expeditions. Here can also be found specialized camps for processing game.

Fig. 3 shows this in more detail with part of research area 2 showing all Neo-Eskimo sites found in 2001 and 2002 on surveys conducted by B. Grønnow, K. Pasda and the author. Large camps are situated at places where further umiaq travel was impossible but dominate in the distinct central parts of the hunting-grounds. These large camps are often associated with large hunting-drive systems, caches, shooting-coverts as well as smaller camps and single sites in their immediate surroundings. In their hinterland small-scale hunting-drives, small groupings of shooting-coverts, used rock shelters and hunters' beds occur. The travel routes to the inland and back are characterized by single rock shelters and hunters' beds where people rested and spent the night.

This picture shows that open-air sites such as summer camps are not distributed randomly in that region but occur at typical locations. Excavation (Grønnow/Meldgaard/Nielsen 1983), dating of structures found during field-work and preliminary results of test excavations (Gabriel et al. 2002; Odgaard et al. 2003) show a certain time depth of some centuries in the use of large summer camps. Therefore the inland region was used more or less continously to hunt caribou which led to the same travel routes and successive occupation of nearly the same localities by different generations sometimes over centuries. This may show that open-air sites in the inland of Central West Greenland, e.g. the large summer camps, but small resting and sleeping places too, were also fixed localities in space and time – a characteristic which is then not an exclusive element of caves and rock shelters.

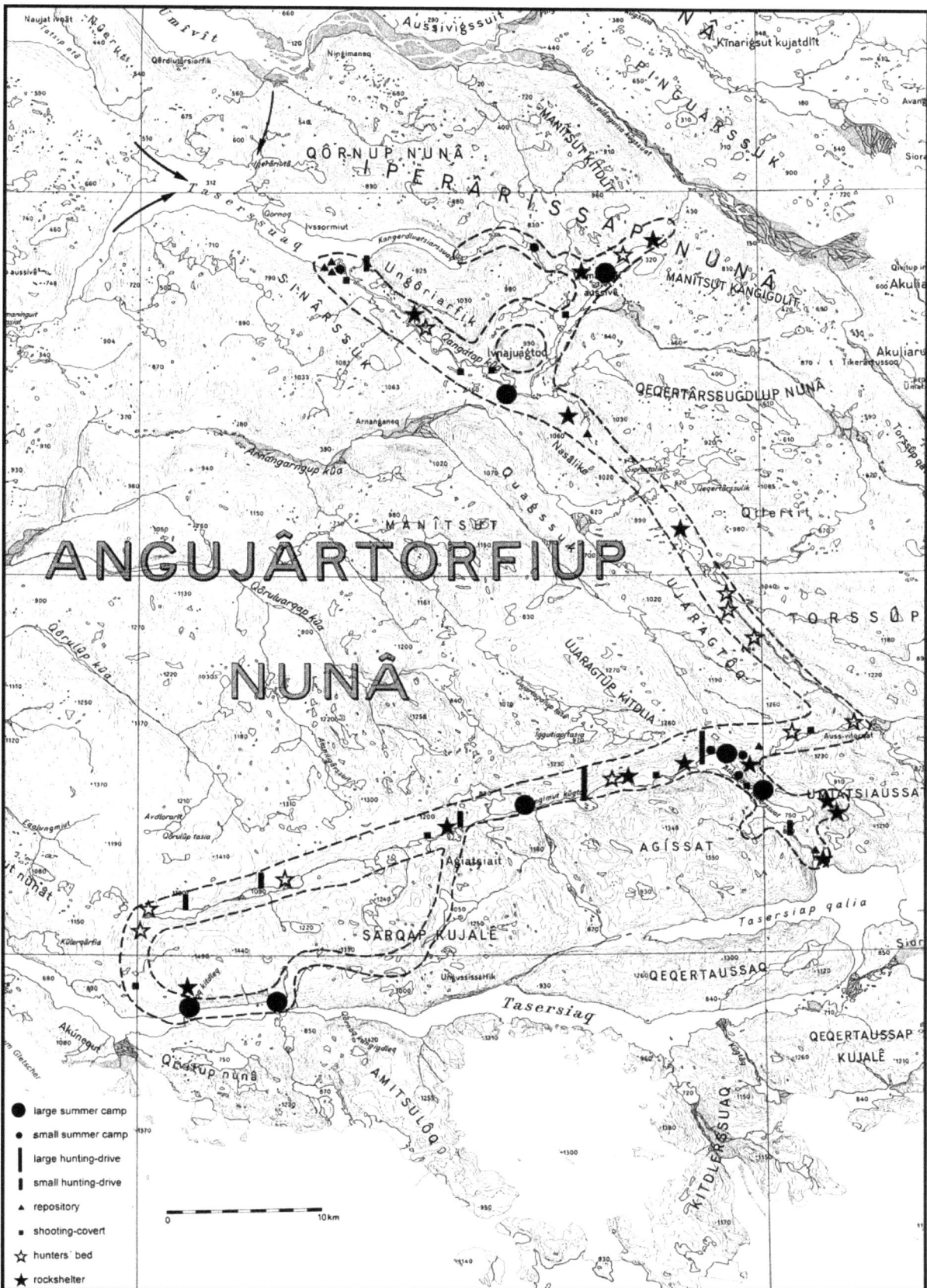

Fig. 3: Sites found in a part of Angujaartorfiup Nunaa in 2001/02 with direction of historic umiaq travel routes (arrows) and surveyed area (broken line). (map made by I. Seeberger (Erlangen) according to field-notes by the author).

Tab. 1: Simplified model of site types and their occurrence in the inland of Central West Greenland (modified after Grønnow 1986 and Pind et al. 1991).

AREA:	FJORD	LAKES AND RIVERS	VALLEY AND PLATEAU	INLAND	HINTERLAND
USE:	travel by umiaq	travel by umiaq	travel by foot	main hunting area	secondary hunting area
SITE:	assembly camp	camp	sleeping and resting places	large camp	sleeping, resting and specialized places

As shown by historic and ethnohistoric sources (Grønnow 1986, 78-79; Grønnow/ Meldgaard/Nielsen 1983; M. Meldgaard 1983) the pattern of inland use changed regularly. The reason for this is to be found in fluctuations of the caribou population in cycles of 60-120 years (Cuyler et al. 2000; M. Meldgaard 1986; Vibe 1967): Extreme caribou scarcity and poor hunting success, which resulted in human starvation, was first recorded in the research areas for the 1760's. In 1815 an increase in caribou numbers was noticed which peaked from 1845-1850. Numbers declined rapidly during the 1850's and reached a minimum in 1860. Caribou remained scarce in the research area until the 1950's. These population fluctuations influence the migrations pattern of caribou (Cuyler et al. 2000, 16) as nearly all caribou stay in distinct areas near the inland ice year round if the population size is low. When the population is at its maximum caribou expand their habitat to the west coast. The caribou population fluctuations led to a discontinuous way of using the inland region, reflected by changes in number and origin of hunting groups, group size and composition, hunting methods and processing of animals as well as differences in the use of sites: M. Meldgaard (1983) has proposed a model where during a caribou population maximum several groups with many people reach the inland region from coastal settlements over even larger distances. They use the large camps in the main hunting area for communal hunting. During a caribou population minimum just a few hunters from a more local area penetrate the inland region, searching actively for single caribou, thus being very mobile and staying for only a short time at a number of different localities. These two general hunting patterns have been altered in the last 300 years by the increasing influence of European whalers and Danish administration and settlements at the coast, by the introduction of new and progressing hunting weapons as well as by dependence on exchange systems between regions. This was demonstrated at the excavation in Aasivissuit, a large summer camp in research area 1 (Grønnow/Meldgaard/Nielsen 1983, 30-32, 53-54, 86-87): In the 13th and 14th century the site seems to be visited only briefly and irregularly by small hunting groups which took caribou with bow and arrow using stalking or shooting-coverts. In the 15th and 16th century hunting methods were the same but frequencies of occupation increased. The most extensive use of the site was between 1650 and 1750, connected with a high caribou-population and the beginning of Danish colonisation. Now caribou were hunted by using the hunting-drive systems in an organized and communal way by many families from different parts of the west coast. As caribou population crashed in the second half of the 18th century and Greenlanders experienced diseases, this use of the inland region came to an end. In the first half of the 19th century the number of caribou increased again and at this time the inland region was again visited by many hunters but now only by groups from a more local area. As guns were now generally used hunting was done on a more individual scale (see: R. Petersen 2003, 54) with shooting-coverts and, sometimes, with small-scale hunting-drives. As caribou populations reached a new low-point after 1850 hunters came inland only sporadically. They did not stay in the larger summer camps for long but used all localities of the region for short stays while searching for the few caribou spread over the whole area and stalking them individually with their technically better guns. At that time Rink (1877, 232-241) described a couple which walked over 100km in several weeks to hunt inland and transport ten caribou back to the settlement at the coast. With a minor caribou increase around 1900 the large summer camps were occupied by hunters and their families again but group size did not reach the same level as 200 years before. With the increasing influence of commercial fishing at the coast in the first half of the 20th century (H.C. Petersen 1986a,

261) this traditional way of caribou-hunting came to an end.

The discontinuous elements of inland use by Greenlanders have important implications for archaeological structures. Obviously, new houses of different forms and size were built in the tradition of the home area of groups arriving from different regions of the West coast (Gulløv 1997; Odgaard et al. 2003). But the function of a site also changed according to the actual nature of inland-use (Grønnow 1986, 78; Grønnow/Meldgaard/Nielsen 1983, 88), so what had been a main summer camp of a large group over several weeks was, some years later, used merely for an overnight stay by just a few individuals - and vice versa. These differences in site use resulted in the alteration of structures built during a previous occupation, e.g. by reducing the space of a large tent-house to use it as a hunters´ bed (Grønnow 1986, 78; Grønnow/Meldgaard/Nielsen 1983, 56; Pasda 2002, 340-341; 350), by building caches or graves inside tent-houses or by taking the stones of older structures to build new ones (Gabriel et al. 2002; Grønnow/Jensen 2003, 169; Odgaard et al. 2003).

The role of caves and rock shelters in the general settlement and subsistence pattern of the research area can be discussed against this background of the results of inland landscape use. Using his ethnographical knowledge the archaeologist B. Grønnow (1986, 72; Pind et al. 1991, 45-56; Secher et al. 1987, 55, 58) interprets archaeological structures and finds in rock shelters as having been used by a small group or few individuals during a brief stay while travelling from the fjord to the inland hunting areas (and back) as well as in the far hinterland of the main hunting areas. In consideration of the changing human subsistence pattern mentioned before one can propose a further argument: Caves and rock shelters may have always been used independently of caribou population fluctuations, each time with the same goal (as resting and sleeping places during travel or caribou-hunts) and the same group size and composition (few individuals). In times with lots of caribou and dominant cooperative hunting around large summer camps rock shelters were used by small groups sporadically and only in the case of secondary, short and small-scale subsistence expeditions (Fig. 4 above). In decades with low caribou population the inland region was used only by very mobile, small groups. These hunters again used rock shelters for a brief stay only, to search for the dispersed caribou in a large area (Fig. 4 below). In chapter 3.2 the material record in rock shelters is analyzed to discuss this supposition.

To sum up, in the research area caves and rock shelters seemed to be spatially fixed localities of a landscape well known by its human users. The localities are known in their geographical position, as is also shown by names for sites, their relation to other sites and for their site-specific characteristics which made their use advantageous or not during a certain situation. Open-air sites share these characteristics with naturally confined localities. It is supposed that the function and use of caves and rock shelters remained the same and was independent of changes in the general land-use patterns of the last centuries.

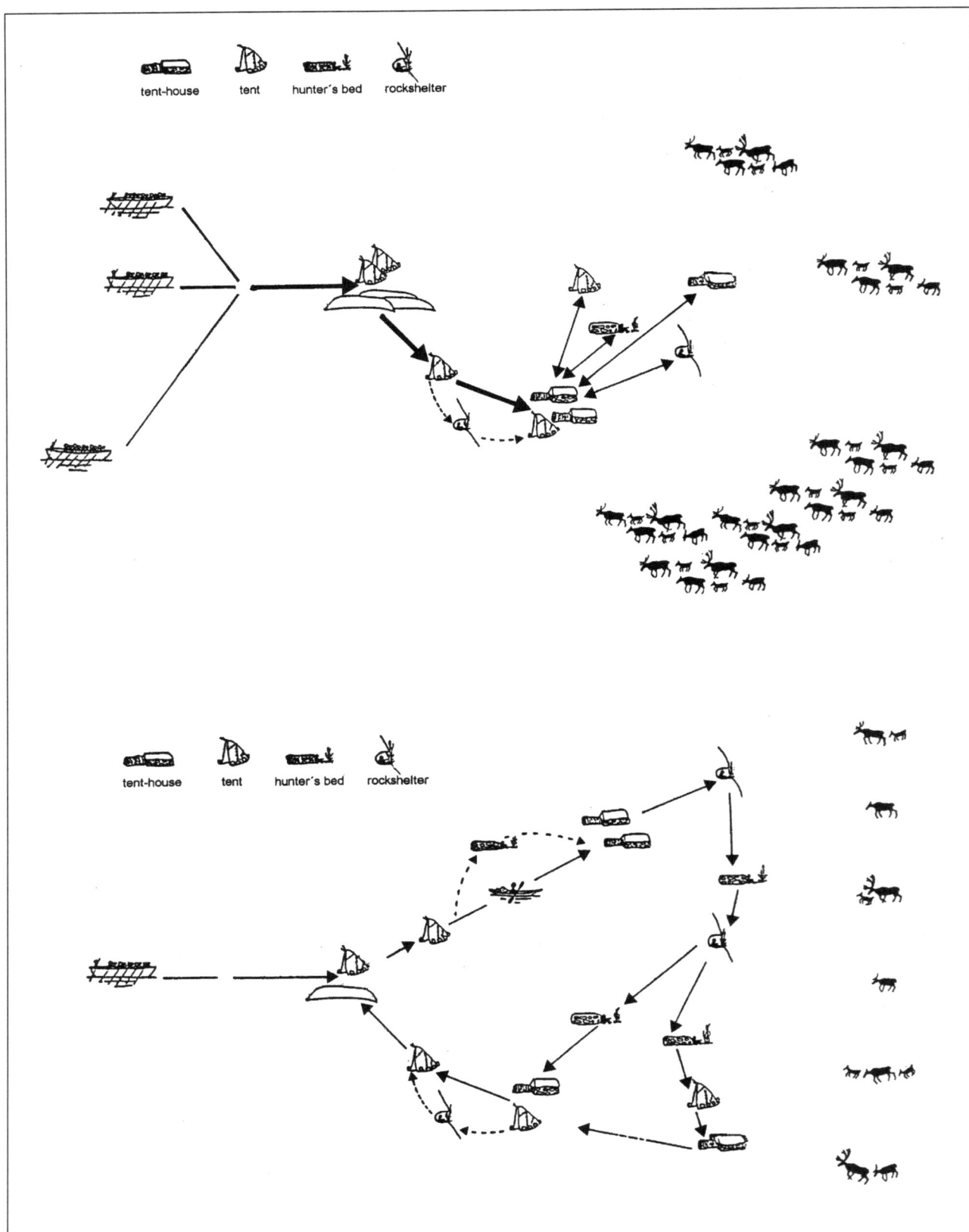

Fig. 4: Spatial behaviour and site use in the inland of Central West Greenland during caribou population maximum (above) and minimum (below) (changed figure after Pind et al. 1991: fig. 6.4).

3. Naturally confined localities in West Greenland

3.1 Variability in the use of caves, rock shelters and boulders

A typical characteristic of the research area is the occurrence of boulders measuring from 1m³ to several meters in diameter up to the size of a European house. Boulders are so numerous (Fig. 5) that counting and statistical comparison of used and unused boulder-overhangs, even in small areas, seemed absurd. Often boulders cover hollows above the earth. Sometimes hollows up to several metres in length could be observed in the debris of rock-falls or frost-cracked rocks (e.g. Pasda 2001, Abb. 6); these could have provided room for many persons but where no archaeological record was present. Deep caves, as defined by Trimmel (1968), do not exist in the research area. Therefore only the use of *"exogene caves"* (Lowe/Walker 1999, 127) - like rock shelters - could be investigated. However, 'real', endogene caves exist in Greenland, e.g. in the inland part of the Nuuk area where larger caves with stone walls and place for 15-20 people occur (Gulløv 1983, 162, 165, 173, 183-184). An occupation area protected by a natural roof can be a reason for using this locality. Nevertheless, the importance and perception of a place is often not recognizable by an archaeologist when human presence does not produce a material record or when the material record is not preserved (e.g. Sommer 1991, 59-61): e.g. on one site (Fig. 6) only three cartridges show human presence at the eastern side of a 2m high boulder. Without these cartridges it is impossible to detect an assumed very short use of the boulder, maybe as a natural hunting-blind or wind-protected hunting-stand. All other finds around this locality, animal bones and dens, have no connection with this human use. The following pages describe the different use of boulders, rock-overhangs and hollows in the research area in West Greenland. Examples found in the field are given, together with references found in different published accounts concerning mainly Greenland. Rock shelters and boulders supposed to be used by Europeans (e.g. M. Petersen 2002) or Norse (e.g. Berglund 2002; Geldager/Hansen/Gleie 2002) are not taken into consideration.

Shooting-coverts and hunting stands (Grønnow/Meldgaard/Nielsen 1983, 45-49) can often be found in the vicinity of large summer camps as well as distant from these in certain topographical situations like passes or narrow bottleneck-like areas, or next to a well-trodden caribou path on an open plain. They occur sometimes as a single structure, sometimes in groups of several shooting-coverts. Shooting-coverts are typically small semicircular or linear built rock wall constructions of 1-3m in length. Sometimes hunting-blinds are connected with *inussuit* of hunting-drive systems which are described below. If a large boulder occurs in a useful topographical situation it would be included in constructing a shooting-covert. As an example Fig. 7 shows an approximately 50cm high wall made of five stones below the overhanging side of a 1,2m high boulder. More shooting-coverts and *inussuit* can be found in the immediate surrounding of that site. Comparable sites have been described from other areas in Greenland: Near a hunting-drive in the Tasermiut-Fjord in South Greenland squared stone walls are built against large boulders (Porsild 1920, 308). At the end of the Saputit-Fjord at the Nugssuaq-Peninsula Nellemann (1969/70) describes a 600m long hunting-drive with 27 meat-caches, 20 hunting-blinds and sleeping-places. The published figure shows at least two *"rock shelter*[s], *closed by a stone wall; presumably "bedroom" for hunters"* (Nellemann 1969/70, 136). On the island Kulusuk in the Amassalik-Fjord in East Greenland a hunting-drive exists with a boulder lying further away. Thalbitzer (1914, 405) writes that this boulder could have been used as a hiding-place of the hunter who informed the others, hidden behind hunting-stands, about the arrival of caribou.

Fig. 5a: Landscape in the inland of West Greenland (research area 1).

Fig. 5b: Landscape in the inland of West Greenland (research area 2).

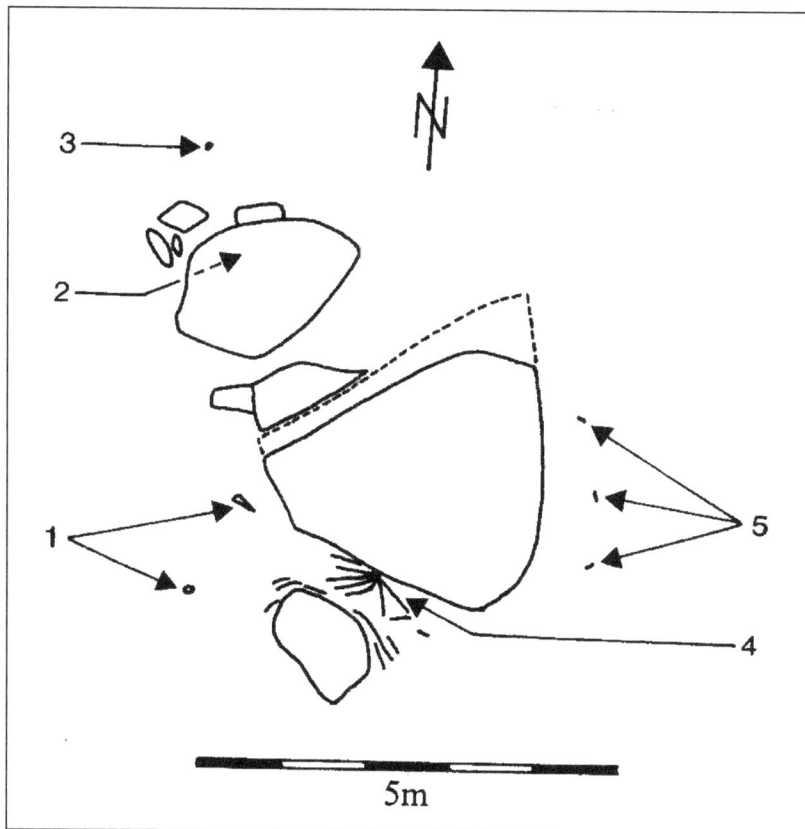

Fig. 6: Boulders (site 9 in Pasda 1999) with proximal tibia and epiphysis of caribou (1), animal den (2), vertebra of hare (3), dwarf shrub vegetation (4) and ammunition AMA 61 (5).

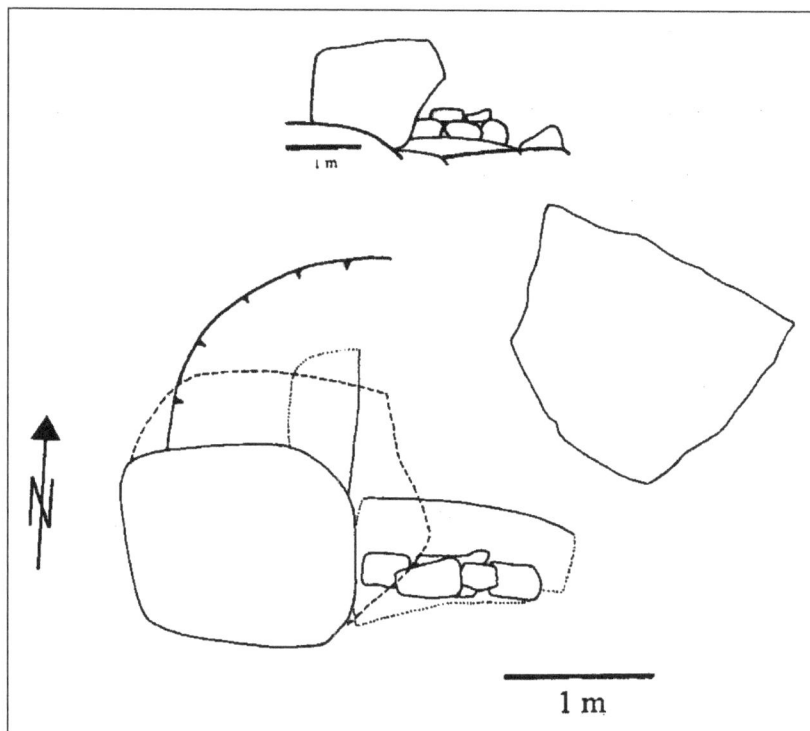

Fig. 7: Shooting-covert (site B16 in Grønnow/Meldgaard/Nielsen (1983). Illustration see Fig. 21.

Fig. 8: Inussuk on top of large boulder (site FM 66V2-IV-133).

Hollows under boulders were used as deposits, e.g. as a cache for equipment. This is reported from the Thule area (Appelt 1999, 31; Appelt et al. 1998, 172-174, 181; Grønnow 1999, 43; Holtved 1944, 45; 1967, 28) and from Angujaartorfik (Kapel 1996, 124) in research area 2 (Fig. 1). Sometimes the bottom of the hollow is covered with stone slabs and the boulder marked by a stone lying on top (Appelt et al. 1998, 181). Caches were built onto large boulders in Palaeo-Eskimo times in northern Greenland (Grønnow/Jensen 2003, 66, 104, 205-206). Several stones lying on top of each other on a large boulder to signify caches nearby have also been found in research area 2 (Fig. 8). Repositories under large boulders can be found in the surrounding of large summer camps, e.g. Aasivissuit. The openings are closed with small stones to protect a narrow chamber containing dry meat, clothes, tools or strings against ravens or polar fox (Grønnow/Meldgaard/Nielsen 1983, 50). Structure D1 from Aasivissuit (Fig. 9), described by Grønnow/Meldgaard/Nielsen (1983, 50) above the remains of tent-houses, can be shown as an example: A 2m high boulder is lying with its western side on some smaller stones. Large openings are closed with slabs (Fig. 9: vertically hatched). In the hollow were found caribou bones and an artefact (Fig. 9: 8) together with a bucket with a turned lid which was covered by stones (Fig. 9: 7).

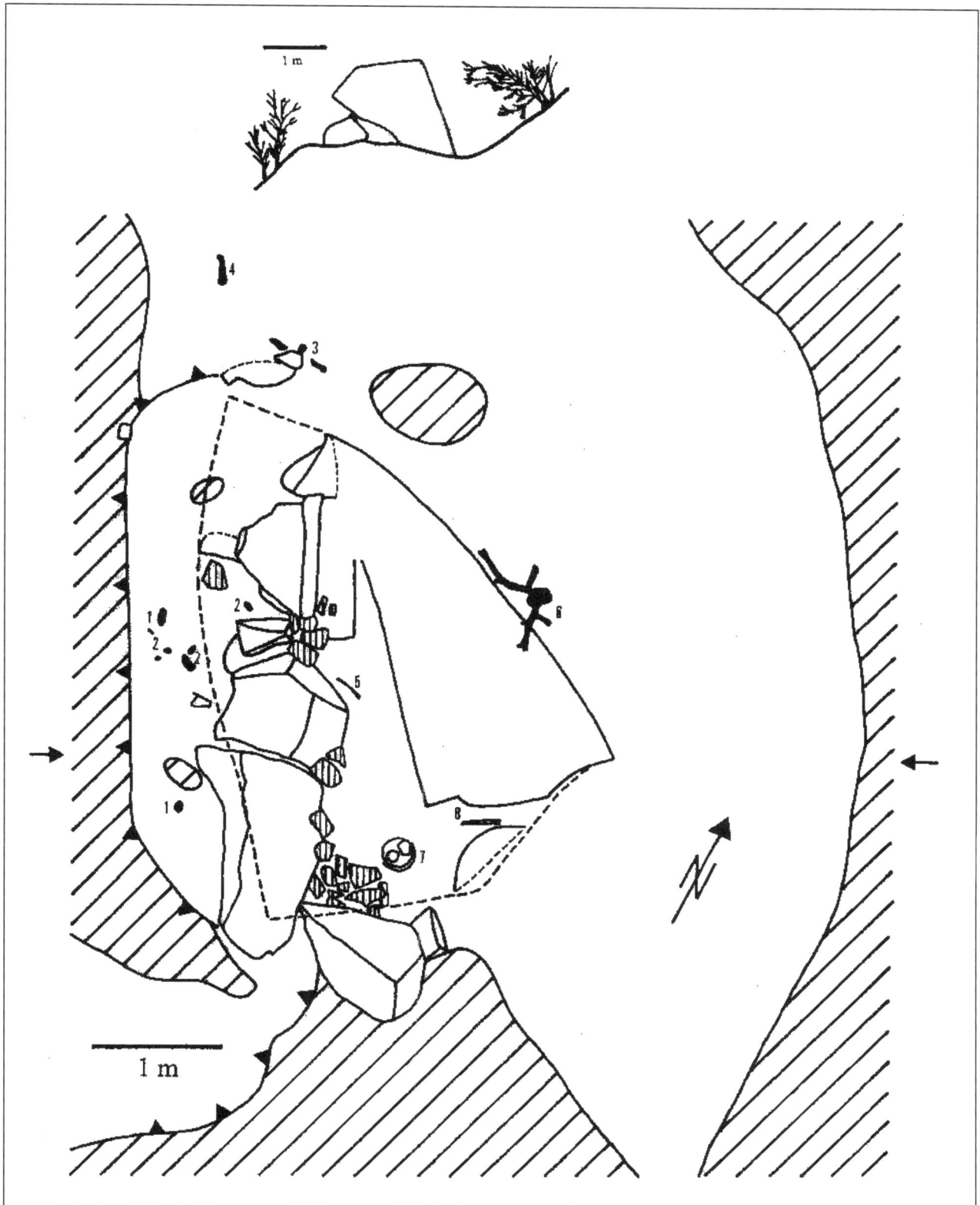

Fig. 9: Repository (site D1 in Grønnow/Meldgaard/Nielsen 1983) with natural rock (white), closing-stones (vertical hatching), dwarf-shrub vegetation (oblique hatching), caribou dung (1), carpal, phalanx, rib fragment, several long-bone fragments of caribou (2), tibia fragment and distal femur of caribou (3), 4 complete caribou metacarpus (4), caribou rib-fragment (5), caribou cranium with sawed antlers and chewing-marks (6), aluminium-bucket (7) and saw-blade (8).

These deposits can also be found at other localities, e.g. where umiaqs and sea-fearing equipment was left behind in order to travel further inland by foot. Such a place is at the eastern end of Lake Tasersuaq (Grønnow/Meldgaard/Nielsen 1983, 24). Here, under a rock wall several deposits were found in 2x1m large hollows below coarse frost-cracked rock-debris (Fig. 10: 71-73). The chambers of the deposits are built by neatly closing natural openings with up to 80 small stones (Fig. 10 below). The bottom of the deposits was covered with twigs. Another deposit was visible at the front on open-ground (Fig. 10: 74). Some meters to the west a small rock shelter (Fig. 10: 70) was also documented (Pasda 2002, Abb. 11).

Hollows under boulders were also used for storage of hunted game: In 18th century West Greenland the storage of dry meat and fish under boulders with stone walls is mentioned by Israel (1969, 75). The same is described by Holm (1914, 131), Thalbitzer (1914, 676) and R. Petersen (2003, 261, 293) from East Greenland and by Steensby (1910, 309) from the Thule region. In the research area meat caches are described by Grønnow/Meldgaard/Nielsen (1983, 49-50): They consist of a central, 50-100cm long chamber which is open today to reveal 30-60cm high walls built out of ten up to several hundred stones. Often meat caches are situated at windy spots, sometimes large natural boulders are included in their construction (Fig. 11).

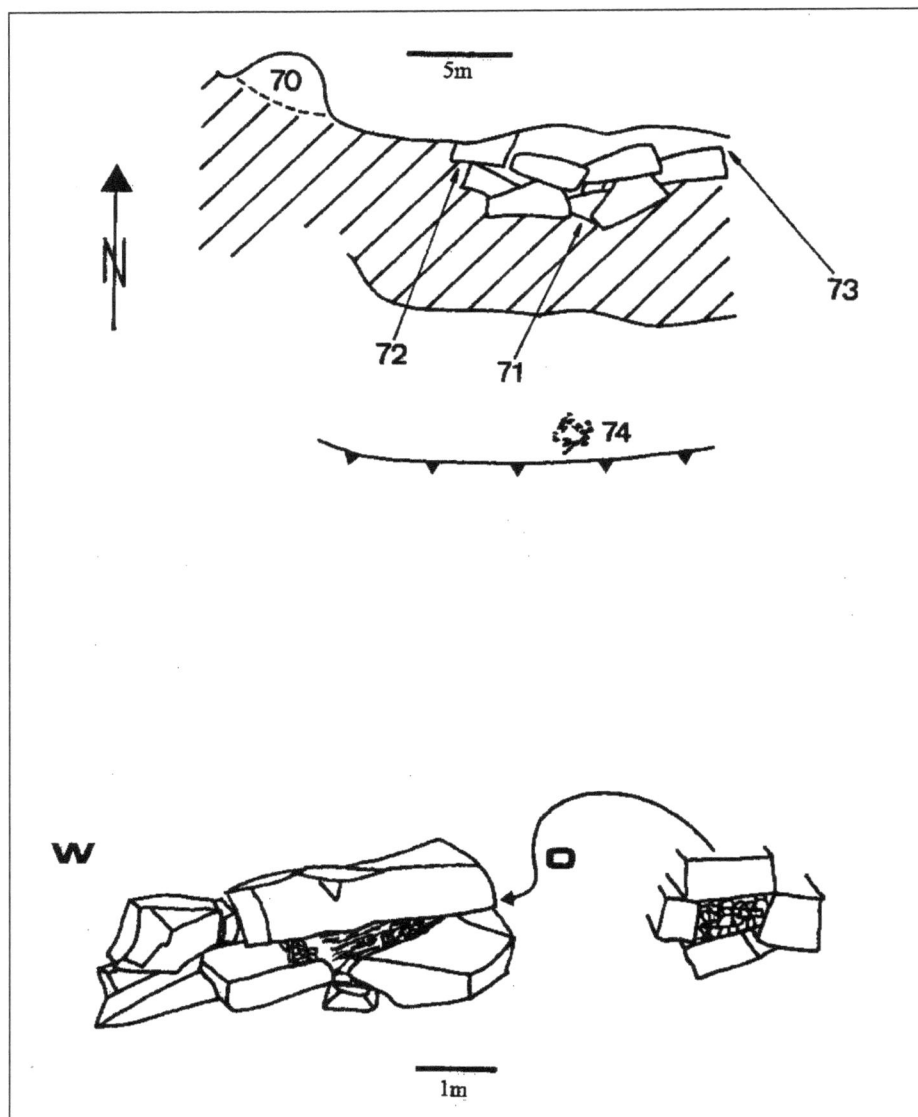

Fig. 10: Deposits (71-73) in hollows under large boulders (sites 70-74 in Pasda 2000).

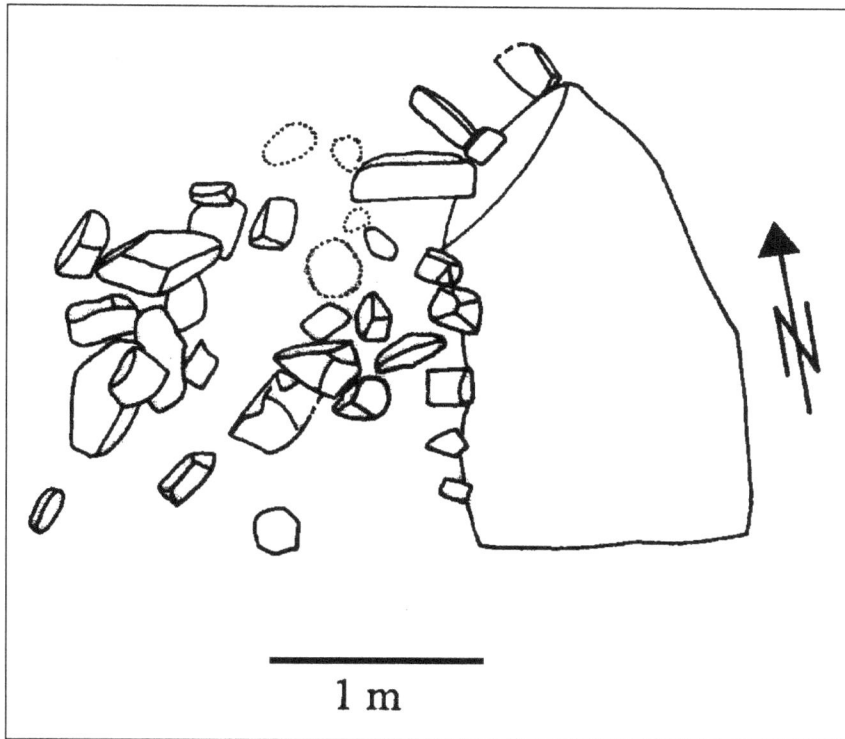

Fig. 11: Meat cache beside a natural boulder (site 31 in Pasda 1999).

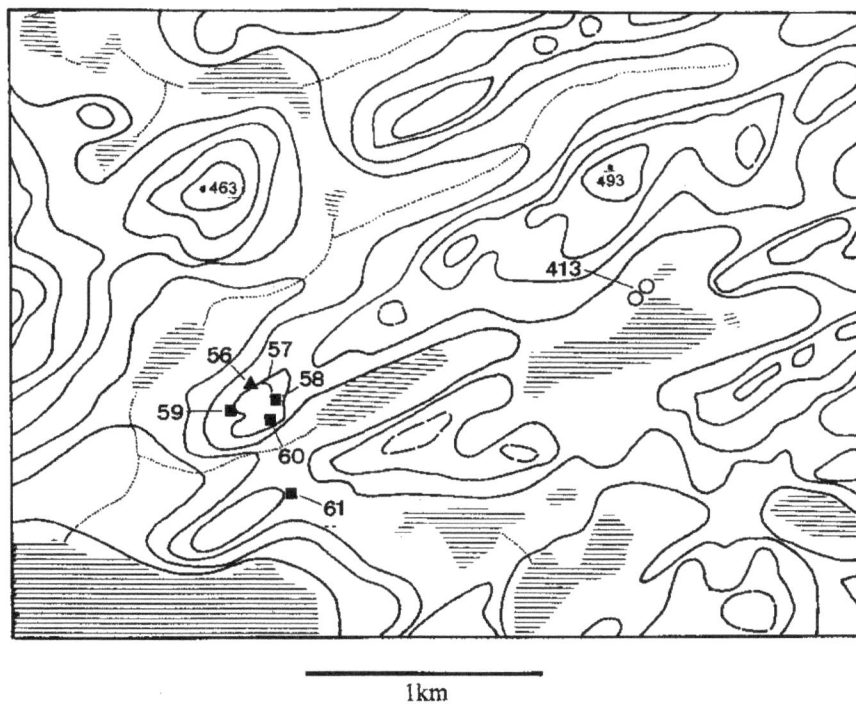

Fig. 12: Small caribou hunting-drive system (sites 56-61 in Pasda 2000; no. 413 = site 413 in Pind et al.1991) with inussuit (58-61), shooting-covert (57), rock shelter (56), tent rings (413), equidistance 25m, lakes (hatched) and creeks (pointed).

In the research area *inussuit* (singular: *inussuk* = "human-like") are described by Grønnow/ Meldgaard/Nielsen (1983, 41-42) as a single stone or several stones piled on top of each other. Sometimes several *inussuit* can be found in linear arrangements which represent organized features of caribou-hunting drive systems. These *inussuit* can present a human-like form (Grønnow/Meldgaard/Nielsen 1983, Fig. 40) or can be altered to that by applying turf or string (Rosing 1988). Sometimes stones or slabs have been artificially layered on top of large natural boulders (Grønnow/Meldgaard/Nielsen 1983, Fig. 41). Sometimes shooting-coverts with or without *inussuit* occur isolated in the landscape, in some cases several days journey far away from large hunting-camps (Grønnow/Meldgaard/Nielsen 1983, 45-49).

At isolated places large natural boulders have also been used. As an example, can be mentioned sites 57-61 (Fig. 12), discovered during 2000. They are situated far away from the next large summer camp and approximately 1,5km west of two tent-rings (Fig. 12: 413) discovered by Pind et al. (1991, 117, 120). Situated on a hill are three *inussuit* (Fig. 12: 58-60) and a shooting-covert (Fig. 12: 57). Eleven stones have been placed on top of a natural boulder which has an overhang to its northern side (Fig. 12: 56; 13). Maybe this is a collapsed *inussuk* (Grønnow/Meldgaard/Nielsen 1983, 41), a shooting-covert or, as this locality offers a good overview across the valley below, an observation point with stones piled on top of each other as an additonal protection against the wind. On the next hill to the south (Fig. 12: 61) a small *inussuk* built with two stones on top of a 1m high natural boulder can be seen from a distance of several kilometres. Possibly this single *inussuk* was a marker *inussuk* as mentioned by Grønnow/Meldgaard/Nielsen (1983, 45) from the Aasvissuit area. A similar statement was made by Mathiassen (1928, 97) for the eastern Canadian Arctic. In research area 2 many single head-sized boulders were found on the inland routes known from ethno-historical sources (Thisted 1997, 228-229) in special topographical situations, such as passes, on vast plateaux (Fig. 14a), near the edges of plateaux or where a larger valley is divided into several valleys (Fig. 14b). This may show that frequently used routes were maintained and upgraded as pathways (Zedeño/Stoffle 2003, 63).

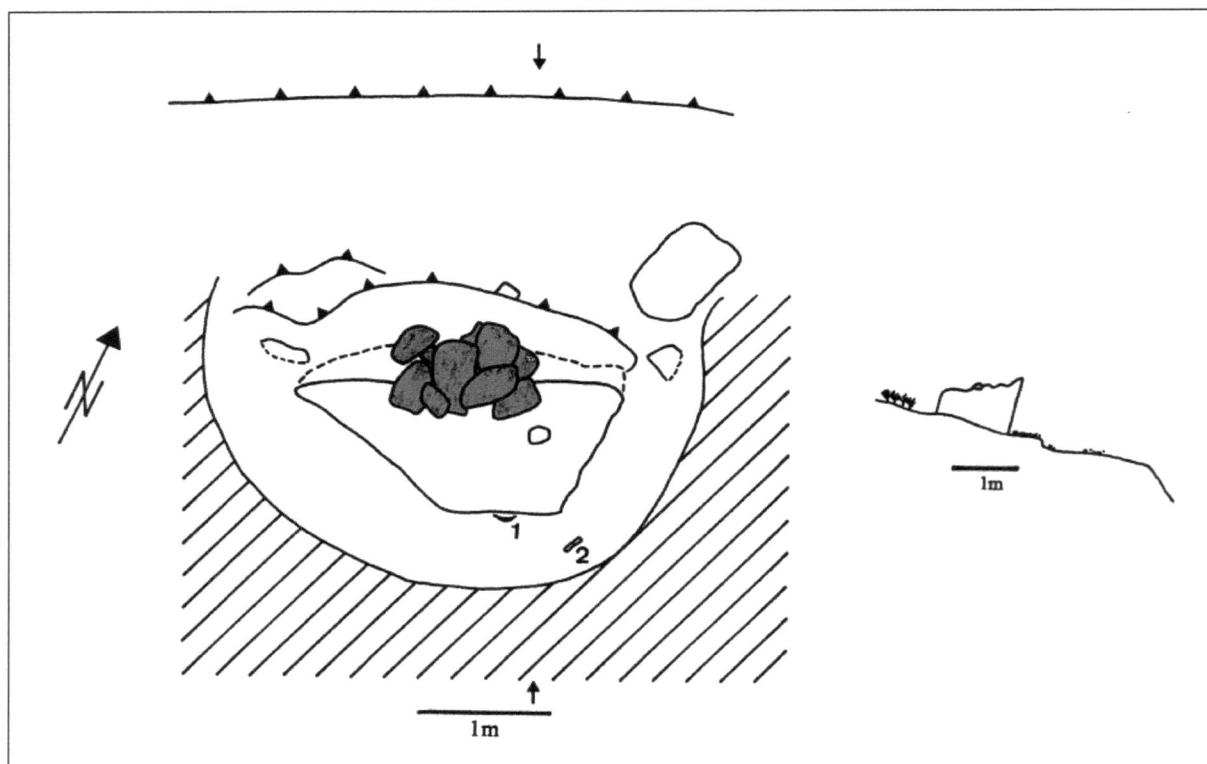

Fig. 13: Archaeological structure (site 56 in Pasda 2000) with boulder (white), archaeological structure (grey), grass (hatched), edge of plateau (line with triangles), musk-ox wool (1), radius fragment of juvenile caribou (2).

Fig. 14a: Inussuk on historic route (site L323/L324 in Gabriel et al. 2002).

Fig. 14b: Inussuk on historic route (site L303 in Gabriel et al. 2002).

Inussuit may not only have been used for hunting and orientation. E. Knuth interpreted an *inussuk* inside a tent ring as a support for the frame of the tent (Grønnow/Jensen 2003, 67). Hallendy (1994; 2000) and Plumet (1985) have documented other reasons to build *inussuit* in the eastern Arctic of Canada; for leaving a message, to mark animal pathes, good hunting-spots or safe ways, to distinctly mark places or objects as useful or to be avoided, as a signal, for navigation and orientation in a landscape, as a symbol of actions, humans, ghosts, myths or stories connected with that spot, in rememberance of dead people, to demonstrate power, out of reverence or because of astronomical reasons. Whether *inussuit* in West Greenland had the same functions is not evident today but this shows that all those various motives for human behaviour cannot be easily seen in the delivered material record.

As marine animals are the main resource of human subsistence in West Greenland the use of caves and rock shelters at the coast needs to be included in the discussion. Beside the dominant hunting of marine mammals and the concentration of settlements at and near the coast and fjords, journeys with boats of several thousand kilometres between East, South and West Greenland were a central part of the social organisation of Greenlanders (Gulløv 1997, 400-407). If caves were used on these journeys is not that clear. Rink (1875, 448) has documented the legend of a long journey by boat where travellers spent the night in caves and rock fissures. And Birket-Smith (1924, 225) wrote about a legend where a woman rested under a boulder while her brothers and sisters, who arrived with a boat, collected berries. According to Trebitsch (1910, 90) the place to stay overnight during a boat journey should have good freshwater, enough firewood and protection against the wind. As the umiaq could easily be drawn up on land, it was not so important whether there were good harbour conditions (R. Petersen 2003, 48). Since the night was spent under their upturned umiaq (e.g. Birket-Smith 1924, 257) or in a tent (e.g. Giesecke 1910; Ostermann 1938, 53) people travelling with an umiaq had not always to rely on caves or rock shelters. Maybe the use of caves and rock shelters was therefore restricted along the coast but dominated in the inland areas. This can be seen in the investigation done by Gulløv (1983, Kort 4) in the Nuuk area where more than half (n=13) of all documented cave and rock shelter sites are situated at least 5km away from the coast. Of these 13 inland caves seven sites represent the only evidence of human occupation of the farmost inland area near the ice cap.

At the coast caves have been used in winter while travelling by dog-sled on the frozen sea. For example, in 1808 Giesecke (1910, 113) used a cave in the rock wall named Skarvefield on Disko-Island for a rest to make tea during a sled-trip. In winter this cave is also used during fishing and hunting trips on the sea ice, in summer it cannot be used due to the high surf near the coast and the steep incline of the rock wall (Giesecke 1910, 81-82). A similar report is given by Holtved (1967, 33) from the Thule area, where the Pakitsoq cave is often used during sled-trips. It can only be used in winter when the frozen sea makes access possible. Due to a sudden ice break-up, sleds and dogs have to be left behind and people have to climb the wall above to be save (Holtved 1967, Fig. 22). In the Thule area overnight stays by walrus hunters in small sandstone-caves on Saunders Island are mentioned (Holtved 1967, 33). Steensby (1910, 287-288) makes a general statement on overnight stays in caves and rock shelters due to bad weather during sled journeys and kayak trips at the coast of the Thule area. In the Uummannaq region of northern West Greenland Giesecke (1910, 311) reported and used two other caves while travelling by sled. One cave was used as a sleeping place, the other for cooking. Further north, in Upernavik, the group with which Giesecke (1910, 320) travelled in 1811 made a rest when consuming a meal in a cave. In this large cave named Karosuk, which is accessible only in winter when the sea is frozen, two tents where erected (Giesecke 1910, 320).

Several references to the use of boulders near coastal settlements are known: Mathiassen (1936a, 34-35) described the settlement Eqalungmiut in South-East Greenland where the people of the Skjoldungen area aggregated for fishing, e.g. in the early 19th century 200-250 people in up to 30 tents. Several tent-rings, a grave and a *"curious sleeping-shelter"* (Mathiassen 1936a, 34) under a large boulder were found. Under the boulder overhang a small wooden vessel was found together with parts of a harpoon, an iron-blade, a scraper, a spoon made of bone, seven pendants of bone and shell, an object of ivory, a needle-case and toy-lamps and vessels, but the context of these objects from the 17-18th century is not that evident from this report. The caves, rock shelters and rock-crevices reported by Holtved (1944) from the Thule area are situated near winter settlements which were the focus of his study. He described e.g. a cave closed with stones (Holtved 1944, 82) and two rock-clefts with a roof made out of caribou antler and turf (Holtved 1944, 62). From Northeast Greenland are reported the remains of a deposit or a shelter under an overhanging wall (Thostrup 1917, 232-233) and 1-4m² large structures with rock walls under boulder overhangs (Glob 1935, 38; Thostrup 1917, 286-287, 294, 324, 328, Pl. III). Amdrup (1909, 317) described *"a small covered chamber built up the side of a perpendicular rocky wall"* with wood, waste from wood-working and parts of umiaqs and kayaks. This structure was situated near a well preserved house and is interpretated by Amdrup (1909, 318) as a workshop. Meat caches in natural hollows, under boulders, in rock-clefts or built onto boulders or rock walls are also reported from coastal regions (Birket-Smith 1917, 14; 1924, 131, 387-388; Johnson 1933, 14, 18, 63-64; Larsen 1938, 23, 27; H.C. Petersen 1986b, 173-175; Thostrup 1917, 229, 266, 271; Rink 1875, 8). Closing caves with stone walls was necessary to prevent dogs from entering or the accumulation of snow by blowing wind which could spoil the contents of meat (R. Petersen 2003, 261). In the Upernavik area deposits left by seal hunters are today situated on small islands where sometimes whole seals are put into hollows in the 6-8m high rock walls (Le Mouël 1978, 133-135). From East Greenland Ostermann (1938, 39) reported the drying of meat of sharks by hanging it on steep rock walls.

At the coast large boulders have been also used as marker-points. Mathiassen (1930, 154) reported small tower-like *inussuit* built out of several stone-slabs on large, sometimes more than 2m high, natural boulders on the highest points of the two neighbour island Inugsuk and Tartoq in the Upernavik area. Holtved (1944, 62) from and Thostrup (1917, 212-214; 328) also described stones piled on top of each other on large boulders in North Greenland and Northeast Greenland respectively.

Some details about the use of boulders can also be found in the literature: e.g. fox-traps built out of head- and fist-sized stones (see: Meldgaard/Rosing/Hansen 1971, 82; M. Meldgaard 1997, Fig. 3), sometimes on large natural boulders (Thostrup 1917, 199-200; Glob 1935, 27) or on graves (Thostrup 1917, 203). To keep things, e.g. fur and skin, away from dogs, these things were left on large and high boulders (Degerbøl 1936, 35).

Grummesgaard-Nielsen (1997) and Andreasen (2003) summarize the different burial-customs of Neo-Eskimo in Greenland: Among these caves, boulder-overhangs, and rock-clefts have been used to bury the dead. Alternatively stone-covered chambers were built onto large natural boulders (Fig. 15). This is known from all areas of Greenland (e.g. Degerbøl 1936, 37; Giesecke 1910, 422; Glob 1935, 19; Grønnow/Jensen 2003, 312; Hansen/Meldgaard/Nordqvist 1991, 58, 136-139; Hansen/Gulløv 1989; Hjarnø 1974; Johnson 1933, 14, 18; Koch/Felbo 1994; Larsen 1934, 67; 1938, 20, 32; J. Meldgaard 1953; Mathiassen 1930, 158, 173; 1931, 29, 46, 52; 1934, 62-69, 147; 1936a, 43-44; 1936b, 33, 64, 103-113; Nyegaard 1995; Rink 1875, 123, 134, 408; Robert-Lamblin 1997, 266; Sørensen/Lynnerup 2003). Maxwell (1985, 158-159) gives an account of human burials in caves from Palaeo-Eskimo times in Newfoundland. In Greenland Neo-Eskimo graves often occur near settlements. Sometimes caves and rock shelters with graves lie directly beside other localities, e.g. places used for an overnight-stay or as a meat cache (Mathiassen 1936b, 103). In general the dead were buried in clothes, often with tools or food (Andreasen 2003, 14): In more than half of the approximately 50 graves from AD 1650-1850 documented by Hjarnø (1974) grave-additions such as hunting-tools, parts of sleds or kayaks, manufacturing-tools, vessels, needle-cases, wooden dolls etc. have been found. Often skeletons with intact clothing (Birket-Smith 1924, 66-67) have been reported from graves in caves and rock shelters, resulting from the good preservation of organic material (R. Petersen 1966/67, 261) by a natural freeze-drying process in the arctic climate (Andreasen 2003, 14). Grave-additions can occur in the grave itself or in rock-clefts nearby (Birket-Smith 1924, 65; Mathiassen 1936b, 56, 64). Nyegaard (1995) mentions a human body with dog remains under a huge stone mound at the entrance of a cave in South Greenland. Often accounts are made of complete or single parts of a kayak in a grave (Birket-Smith 1917, 7-8; 1924, 65; Glob 1935, 33; H.C. Petersen 1997, 74; R. Petersen 1966/67, 263), a vessel which in Greenland was owned and used by one person (R. Petersen 2003, 44). For example H.C. Petersen published the approximately 300-400 years old and 5m long Eqalulik-kayak which was found in 1971 with lance, harpoon and throwing-board 35km north of Sisimiut in *"a damp mountain crevice (...) next to a heathen grave"* (H.C. Petersen 1986b, 56-57). Sometimes kayak-like structures were built out of

Fig. 15: Grave chamber under boulder (site L604 in Odgaard et al. 2003).

stone (e.g. Koch/Felbo 1994). Mathiassen (1931, 52) described the opening, disturbance and looting of graves and their secondary use, e.g. as meat cache. The best-known burial on Greenland is from Qilakitsoq in northern West Greenland (Hansen/Gulløv 1989; Hansen/Meldgaard/Nordqvist 1991; Lynnerup 2003), where two burials with five and three well-preserved mummies from the 15th century have been found in a small bay on the northern side of Nuussuaq-Peninsula. The burials were situated below an overhanging rock wall approximately 200m away from winter-houses. The floor of the grave was built out of flat stone-slabs, grass and heather. The single bodies were covered in part with animal-skins or grass, the whole burial was covered with flat stones from the immediate surroundings. Finally, in Greenland there occur carefully built graves without human bodies which may have been built in memory of lost hunters or were built by Greenlanders for themselves but were then not used (Birket-Smith 1924, 65).

Bielawski (1989, 234) quotes E.S. Carpenter who wrote in 1956: *"Wherever they* [Inuit] *go, their surroundings have meaning for them; every ruin, rock, and cleft is imbued with mythical significance."* This sentence serves as just one example for the importance and perception of certain localities which do not yield any material record left by humans. As pointed out above, natural boulders were parts of the humanized landscape fixed in space and time: Jens Rosing told about hunters in Ammassalik who, in 1934, used a certain overhanging boulder as a place to manufacture and repair tools but mainly for telling stories (Pasternak 1999, 57). Mythical beings were connected with certain places too (e.g. Birket-Smith 1924, 221-225), for example with rocks. According to Rink (1875, 37, 461) the underworld, which carried the earth-surface on pillars, could be entered from openings in the sea, through mountain-clefts or from hollows under large boulders. The so called *ignersuit* were beings living in the underground or in rock walls with invisible entrances along the sea (Birket-Smith 1924, 233; Rink 1875, 46, 183, 299; 1877, 204). Different mythical beings lived on the bottom of lakes or inside certain boulders (Birket-Smith 1924, 228; Rink 1875, 48) or could come out of valley- or mountain sides to be dangerous for humans (Rink 1875, 451). On the other hand caves could also be safe places for humans attacked by mythical beings (Rink 1875, 464). During journeys or while passing particular spots gifts were left at certain stones, ice caps or ice-fjords (Rink 1875, 56). Offerings by boat-crews were made at rapids or where stones are close the surface of the water (Birket-Smith 1924, 215, 220). In West Greenland offerings are described on stones, e.g. entire stones being covered with whale-blubber, placing of blubber in small rock-holes or of skin and fish in rock-clefts (Birket-Smith 1924, 444). On Sentry-Island at the west coast of Hudson Bay in Canada a large boulder hung around with goods to promote hunting of sea-mammals is described by Birket-Smith (1948, Abb. 6) and Hallendy (2000, 30-31). But caves have also been used in a spiritual way or to perform magical arts; these places were used by persons who wanted to become *angakoq* or shaman (Birket-Smith 1924, 452; Ostermann 1938, 135; Rink 1875, 456). Such persons spent a certain time in caves in rubbing a small round stone on a larger, flat stone until a spiritual event was experienced (Birket-Smith 1924, 452; Holm 1914, 88; Ostermann 1938, 196; Rink 1875, 58-59). Rink (1875, 451) gives an account of a spiritual experience by a shaman in a cave, while Sonne (1982, 27-28) shows the connection between long stays in caves and spiritual experiences for the Upernavik region. Geerteeraq Dahl told about a spot at the coast of research area 2: *"There is a place they call the place for shamans on the land of Eqalugaarsuit. It is a huge horizontal long rock cave facing east with an opening to the west. Similarly this one is low to the ceiling as well when you have look inside. This one apparently has an entrance like the ones they used to have in peat-houses. But I have not been there myself to see it with my own eyes. Sometimes I think I should go there just to see if the stories are true"* (Hansen/Larsen 2002). In East Greenland places without daylight, e.g. caves or hollows under boulders, were used to make a *tupilak* (Ostermann 1938, 160, 164, 171). This is an artificial figure made out of earth, human, animal or plant remains, an ordinary object, a certain animal or an invisible being made or created by shamans, by women practicing black magics or by ordinary people with magic skills to do evil things to other humans or to kill them (R. Petersen 1964).

Also described are the lifting or throwing of stones for physical exercise (e.g. Rink 1875, 135) or to demonstrate power (e.g. Gilberg 1984, Fig. 11). Stories and legends tell about persons with unusual power who could move enormous boulders (e.g. Danielsen/Rasmussen/Rosendahl 1967, 43). Caves were used as safe places in case of persecution or attack by other humans (Birket-Smith 1924, 233; Rink 1875, 145, 287). An anecdote is reported by Giesecke (1910, 315) about the two caves in the Uummannaq area mentioned above; in 1811 a pair of lovers stayed here for some days to escape from their respective wife and husband as well as from their children.

Caves may have been used permanently in Greenland only under special circumstances. This has to be seen in connection with the *qivitoq* (Birket-Smith 1924, 450-451; Giesecke 1910, 369; Hansen/Meldgaard/Nordqvist 1991, 60; Nansen 1991, 249; R. Petersen 1964, 79-85; Rink 1875, 45, 104; Sonne 1982, 40): This is a person who retreats or is expelled from human society because of various reasons, e.g. unjustified treatment, quarrel, murder, robbery, insanity, waiting for revenge. A *qivitoq* retreats from other humans to live alone in the mountains or in the interior and has strange, eccentric or certain physical abilities such as being fast-footed, or can perform certain magical, sometimes dangerous things, e.g. clairvoyance. It is said that they also lived in caves (see: Thisted 1999, 394), among other places. Therefore finding human bones or burials in naturally confined localities was a proof of the existence of a *qivitoq* (Birket-Smith 1924, 66; Giesecke 1910, 470; Nansen 1991, 249; Ostermann 1921, 146). Fridtjof Nansen (1991), who spent the winter 1888/89 in the Nuuk area after the first recorded crossing of the inland ice, wrote about a *qivitoq*-cave found some years before on the island of Akugdlit. A distinct path led to the entrance of that cave which had a fireplace, a hole to store food, a smooth bed made of moss and remains of dried fish and edible roots. In a smaller cave nearby was found a grave closed with stones over a human corpse clad in furs. Rink (1875, 261) narrates a legend about a *qivitoq* who lived in a cave or hole inside rocks, which was behind a carefully closed entrance covered with caribou skin. Nearby was a deposit with skins and meat. Sometimes this *qivitoq* stayed with his relatives in the cave. The statement of Seth Olsen shows that the difference between a grave, a dwelling and the scene of an accident is quite clear: *"(...) this one place on the very bottom of the fjord, there is a place of storage. The deceased Kristoffer has filled the hole because there was a dead person it it. It was made into a grave. I do not know the reason why the body was there. It could have been a person that was lost, the person was wearing reindeer clothes. The possibility of the person being a qivitoq is out of question because this place is too much in the shadow. (...) there are several reindeer hind limbs in front of it. (...) We are not assuming the person to be a qivitoq. (...) I am assuming the person had an accident or became lost because that area is very hilly and has many cliffs"* (Hansen/Larsen 2002). The same was said by Geerteraq Dahl about Qivittup nunna situated on the coast west of the research area at the Itilleq-Fjord: *"According to the stories I've heard umiaqs used to avoid the place when passing by. The qivitoq apparently lived there. We have been there to have a look at the place to see if the stories had some truth to them. But the place was too small and too low to the ceiling for someone to have lived there. But there were traces of left over [from] animal bones and debris. Of course the place could have changed over time and the rock to the entrance could have been lowered, but now it is unlikely that someone lived there. According to the stories back when they had kayaks, there was enough space inside the cave for the qivitoq's kayak to turn all the way around. The place was situated in such a way that the qivitoq had a view over the water, whereas from the waterfront you could not spot the site [due] to tall grass. Today there is still evidence of man made rock piles near the cliff toward the water"* (Hansen/Larsen 2002).

Some references show the use of large natural boulders to build massive houses (e.g. Degerbøl 1936, 9, fig. 31; Grønnow/Jensen 2003, 68, 174, 186-188, 306-307; Holtved 1944, 41; Mathiassen 1933, 21; 1936b, 33) and tents (e.g. Knuth 1981, 92-94; Thostrup 1917, 233-234, 333, Pl. III). E. Knuth believed that a boulder could support the rear of a tent cover and that the tent skin could have been kept in place by anchor stones now found behind and in front of the boulder which could itself then have functioned as a backrest inside the dwelling (Grønnow/Jensen 2003, 187). In the northern parts of Greenland flagstone pavements and single hearths were built against large boulders by Palaeo-Eskimo (Grønnow/Jensen 2003, 160, 182, 224). In research area 2 historic tent-houses in summer camps were sometimes built in front of or against south-exposed rock walls (Fig. 16a). Grønnow/Meldgaard/Nielsen (1983, fig. 23) show a picture of the tent-house of Peter Rosing from 1923 where entrance and cooking-niche were built up to a large boulder. In the same region tent-houses of the Thule culture were more often built around or onto large, natural boulders (Fig. 16b). An example can also be shown from research area 1 where a small historic summer camp with houses and deposits was discovered in 1999.

Fig. 16a: Remains of historic tent-house in front of south-facing rock wall (site FM 66V2-II-015).

Fig. 16b: Remains of a Thule tent-house (site FM 66V2-II-031).

Fig. 17: Historic summer camp with tent-houses and deposits (site 24 in Pasda 1999), boulders (white), turf wall (black), dwarf-shrub vegetation (hatched), edge of plateau (line with triangles).

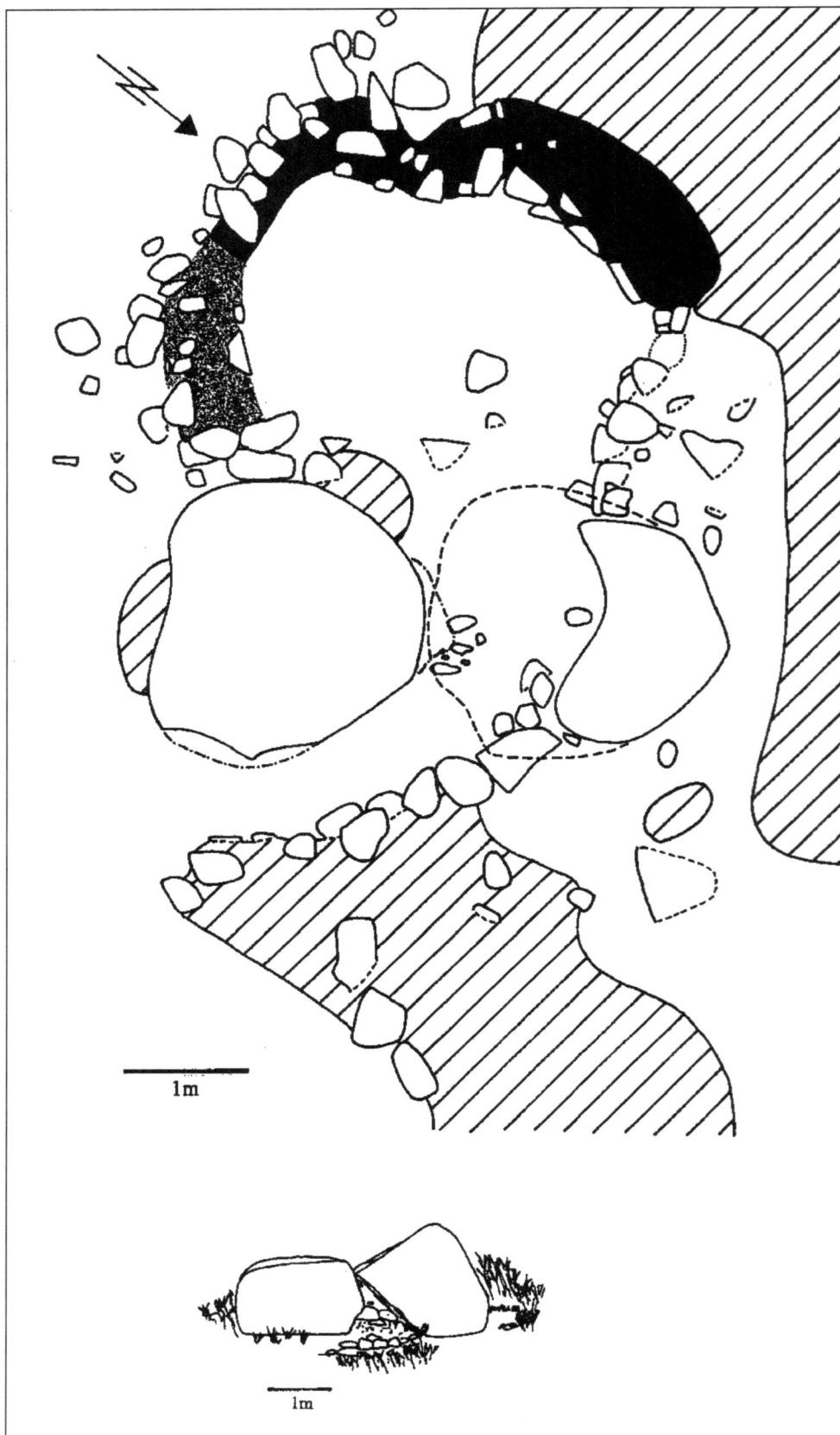

Fig. 18: Tent-house (site 64 in Pasda 2000) built onto two natural boulders (white) with turf-wall (black), indistinct turf wall (grey), dwarf-shrub vegetation (hatched) and edge of plateau (line with triangles).

Structure V (Fig. 17) was built beside a 3m long and 2m high boulder. Here two other tent-houses (Fig. 17: III, IV) have been re-used in later times following construction of smaller walls inside; maybe they were intended to be used not as a tent-house for the whole summer but as a hunters' bed for a short overnight-stay without a roof. At the northern shore of lake Aasivissuit Tasiat in research area 1 a tent-house (Fig. 18) was found in 1990 by Pind et al. (1991, 61, 122). Here two natural boulders of 2m diameter create a 1,1m high and 2,5x1m large natural space onto which was built a round wall of stone and turf with a 3m diameter. If the relatively long entrance-passage to the west is not a functional product of constructing the tent-house onto the boulders this site represents an older Neo-Eskimo house-type (Pind et al. 1991, 65).

3.2 Material record of occupation in rock shelters in the research area

As mentioned in chapter 2, Bjarne Grønnow (1986, 72; Pind et al. 1991, 55, 80; Secher et al. 1987, 55, 58) has combined the archaeological evidence with ethno-historic informations to explain the use of caves and rock shelters in the research area: Naturally confined localities were used as resting and sleeping places by few individuals or small groups during brief stays while travelling inland and back, as well as on minor hunting expeditions in the far hinterland. The archaeological evidence is given in the form of fireplaces, artefacts, smashed marrow-bearing bones and stone walls in rock shelters as well as their topographical location in connection with other sites. Some further ethnographic informations can be added: As shown in chapter 2 by the accounts of Tobias Mouritzen (Grønnow 1986, 78) and Geerteeraq Dahl (Hansen/Larsen 2002), boulders used for overnight stays had place names and built walls. The story of the caribou-hunting couple told by Rink (1877, 234) confirms the short stay, e.g. as the couple stayed two weeks in a cave due to bad weather. Similar observations were made by the German geologist Karl Gripp (1941/42, 41-43) who accompanied some Greenlanders in the hinterland of Nuuk in 1930. The hunters left not only smashed limb bones but scratched their names, initials and the number of the year in the lichen or moss. Real engravings under overhanging walls are not known from Greenland but are documented from Canada (e.g. Arsenault/Gagnon/Gendron 1998). In the Nuuk area certain places have been visited regularly. On one site up to 60 markings from a period of more than 50 years have been found by Gripp (1941/42, 41-43) in form of small pieces of soapstone, flat hammered lead bullets, cartridge cases with notes written on paper and pencil-written caribou antler. These boulders and rock shelters used in 1930 had low walls built out of stones and turf, a ground covered with heather and a roof made out of a tent sheet under which the hunters slept very close to each other to conserve body heat (Gripp 1941/42, 43). There is a detailed description of such a place near the inland ice at 600m a.s.l.: *"(...) zunächst rupften sie, gleich nachdem der Lagerplatz ausgesucht war, Heidekraut aus und ließen es auf den von der Sonne erwärmten Steinen trocknen. Dann bauten sie aus Steinen und Rasen eine Mauer zwischen einer Felswand und einem großen, in geringem Abstand davor gelegenen Stein. Eine zweite, weniger hohe Mauer zogen sie von dem anderen Ende des Steins zum Fels. Der so abgeschlossene Raum war so eng, dass kaum zwei von den Männern darin sitzen konnten. Sie legten ihn mit dem getrockneten Heidekraut aus. Abends packten sie sich dann zu dreien hinein. Der zuletzt einsteigende füllte alle Löcher, insbesondere den fehlenden Teil der zweiten Mauer, mit bereitgelegtem Heidekraut und Steinen bis hinauf in das von uns mitgelieferte Dach aus Zeltunterlage an. Darin lagen sie die Nacht bei 5 Grad Celsius Kälte und waren gegen den Eiswind völlig geborgen. Ihre paktische Kleidung (...) ist bei solcher Lebensweise sinnvoll"* (Gripp 1941/42, 42-44). These Greenlanders built walls of stone and turf to protect a very narrow space under a rock shelter with just enough place for some individuals to crawl in. The same is said by Geerteeraq Dahl (Hansen/Larsen 2002) about the small cave which could be used just by three people crawling in (chapter 2). The Greenlanders accompanied by Karl Gripp slept in their clothes on the floor which was filled with heather and twigs collected and dried outside. The construction served as protection against wind and cold, in the quoted example during a night with -5°C. The remark about sleeping in clothes can also be seen in a picture made by Aron of Kangeq (Thisted 1999, 394). But if the natural characteristics of a rock shelter were suitable no walls were built by its human users: *"(...) our place of retreat was pretty comfortable, situated below a beetling rock, lined with fine grass, and sheltered by a hill like a low wall. So the rain passed by on the outside and we had no need to build up walls"* (Rink 1877, 234). One can assume that conserving body heat - as seen also by the remark given by Laarseeraq Enoksen (Hansen/Larsen 2002) in chapter 2 - was the determining factor whether or not to build a particular type of construction. For completeness it has to be mentioned that during caribou-hunting it was possible to spend the night in the open in a similar way: *"(...) they use to put dry grass inside their clothes, in order to protect themselves against the cold; but this, no more than any other trouble, is considered by the Greenlanders as a real hardship"* (Birket-Smith 1924, 347).

Overnight stays during summer in the research area might seem to be a pleasure when reading, that research area 1 is the warmest region of Greenland at this season (Willemse 2000, 134) and combining that information with long daylight hours due to northern latitude sunshine (see: Berthelsen/Mortensen/Mortensen 1997, 38). However, the daily variation in temperature of up to 20°C and the daily amplitude of wind velocity at 4-5m/s (see Willemse 2000, Fig. 5.5) has to be borne in mind, together with the annual precipitation, which occurs mainly in summer. In addition, the stable, dry high-pressure periods in summer can change within hours to be followed by days with rain, snow and lower temperatures (Rott/Obleitner 1992). Otherwise, dryness in summer can be reinforced by dry *föhn* and katabatic winds. These winds and short-term weather inversions have a heavy influence, e.g. in winter when a sudden rise of temperature of 10-20°C melts the snow-cover. The use of rock shelters may be dependent on microclimate which can be influenced by snow-cover, ice-cover and also by the temperature of lakes: Snow-cover in general varies from year to year but is thin (<20cm) and normally present from end of September to the beginning of May (Grønnow/Meldgaard/Nielsen 1983, 7; Vibe 1967, 178; Willemse 2000, 129, 135). Lakes can be covered by 1,6m of ice until mid-May (Anderson et al. 2000, 84). Generally ice-melt of low-lying lakes starts in early June and is a relatively rapid process, but, depending on weather conditions, can sometimes still not be complete at the beginning of July (Anderson/Brodersen 2001). After ice-melt the warming of the lakes depends on their locations, altitude, and landscape morphometry (Brodersen/Anderson 2000): Today low-lying lakes warm up faster, earlier and to a higher temperature, e.g. with a maximum temperature of nearly 19°C in early July. Higher lakes remain cold, e.g. with a temperature below 10°C until early August.

Accordering to written sources the equipment of human users of rock shelters is reduced to the most necessary: The couple mentioned by Rink (1877, 232-241) had their clothes and carried small books, a rifle, ammunition and two knifes. The picture made by Aron from Kangeq showed a hunter with a rifle and pouch or bag sleeping in a cave (Thisted 1999, 460). The Greenlanders who were accompanied by Gripp (1941/42) took their hunting-gear but carried the tent and the provisions of the geologists. During summer caribou-hunts in northern West Greenland lasting several days (besides the clothes they wore) the hunters carried (by their own backs) only hunting tools, carrying slings, matches, coffee and tobacco (R. Petersen 2003, 39). Often the kayak was carried on the shoulders for several days during hunts in the hinterland (R. Petersen 2003, 39, 44). As the excavations in Aasivissuit and ethno-historic sources of that region have shown (Grønnow/Meldgaard/Nielsen 1983) kayak, tent, tobacco, pipe, coffee, fire-lighter, provisions and vessels or pots have also been brought into a large camp far inland. Because living inland with the activities of walking, hunting, kneeling, carrying or building puts wear and tear on the equipment, special reinforced trousers and shoes were used (Grønnow/Meldgaard/Nielsen 1983, 32) but sewing equipment and skin patches were also part of the gear (R. Petersen 2003, 39). Nevertheless, items such as needles were found rarely in the research area, as is shown by just two bone needles from the large summer camp Aasivissuit (Grønnow/Meldgaard/Nielsen 1983, 90).

With this information from written sources a look at the archaeological consequences of human behaviour will now be discussed. The main question is: What material record is left due by short stays of a few hunters? The first three examples are from research area 1, the following sites from research area 2.

Approximately 5km east of the large summer camp Qarlissuit (Pind et al. 1991, 69-81) an approximately 4m high boulder was discovered and documented first by Pind et al. (1991, 127) in 1990. The isolated boulder is situated at the top of a 501m high mountain with an excellent view over areas more than 100km away, but the site is also very exposed to wind. At the southwest side lies a 1.0 x 0.75m large, rectangular structure (Fig. 19: horizontally hatched) made of 30-40cm high, upright standing stones. The stones at the northwestern edge seemed to be shifted by geli-/solifluction on the slope with its minor steps. To the northern side musk-ox have produced a significant step (see: C. Pasda 2001, 325). According to Pind et al. (1991, 71) this site is situated near a bottleneck situation where passing caribou seemed to concentrate and could be killed more easily.

Another rock shelter is situated approximately 7km away from the nearest known site. Under the overhanging wall of a 3,5m high boulder only two, 25 and 30cm high, upright standing stones (Fig. 20) have possibly been erected by humans to be used as a small wind-break. A small patch of shattered stones and finer sediment (Fig. 20: 2) may derive from frost (or fire?) phenomena. This site is situated several meters above a some kilometres long, narrow west / east running valley, which seems - to the eyes of a modern Central European non-hunter – to be a good place for hunting.

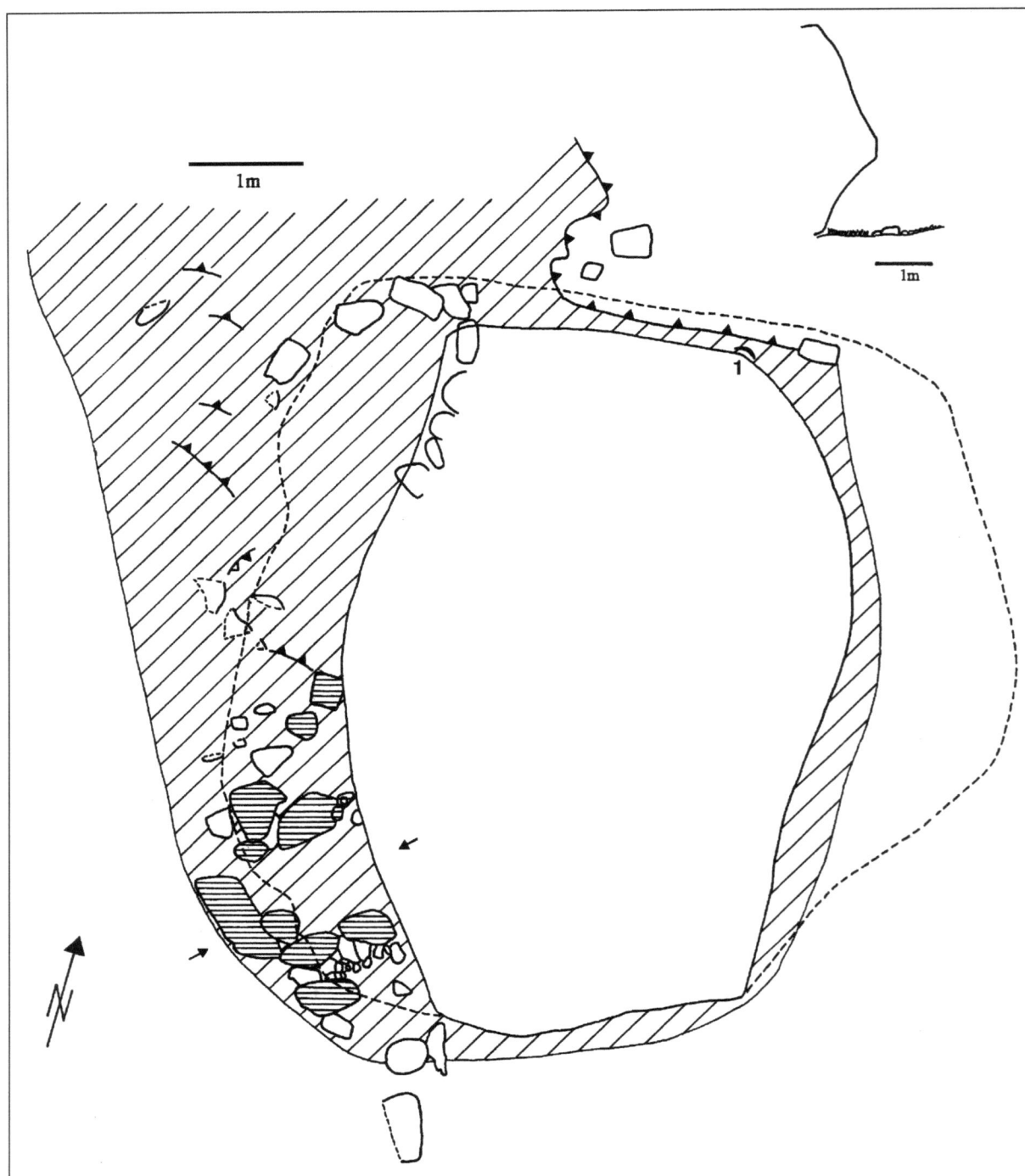

Fig. 19: Boulder with rectangular structure made out of stone (site 80 in Pasda 2000) with musk-ox wool (1), boulder (white), drip-line (broken line), archaeological structure (horizontal hatched), grass vegetation (oblique hatched), edge of plateau (line with triangles).

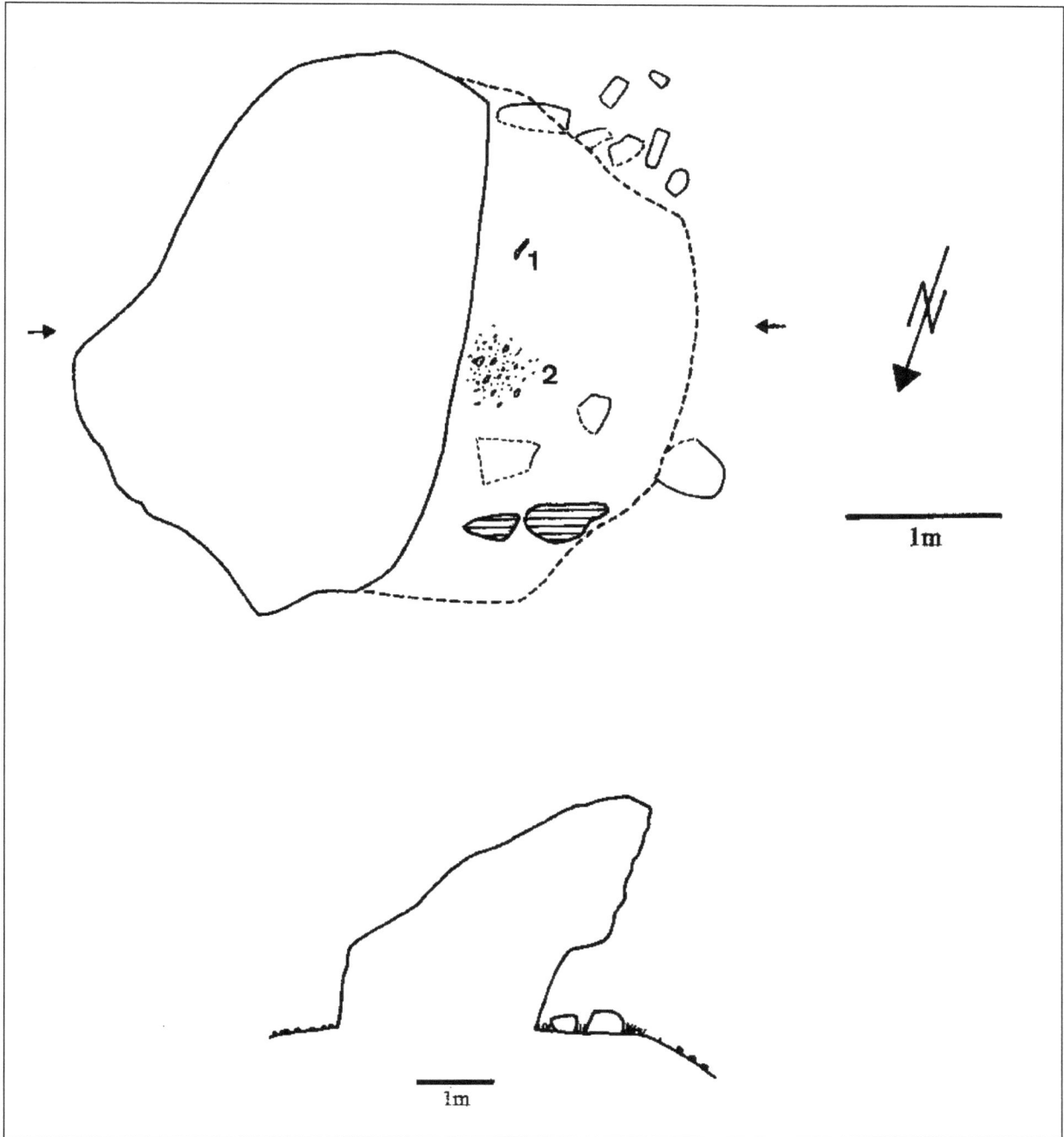

Fig. 20: Boulder with two upright standing stones (site 62 in Pasda 2000) and caribou phalanx (1), fine sediment (2), boulder (white), drip line (broken line) and archaeological structure (hatched).

Grønnow/Meldgaard/Nielsen (1983, Fig. 18) have published a photograph of a sleeping place on a route used while travelling inland by foot: As seen in August 2000 it is an approximately 1m deep and 1,5m wide natural crevice between two boulders with space for three persons. Maybe the crevice was also used as deposit, while staying in a tent some metres away which is today presented by a simple tent ring. But no archaeological finds or structures can be seen inside the crevice.

In the hinterland near the inland ice, some kilometres away from the large summer camps, the structures documented in fig. 21-23 were found. On a very steep slope with many huge boulders an approximately 50cm high, rectangular stone wall built out of some 30 stones was found (Fig. 21a). The stone wall lies between the back of the rock shelter and large natural boulders in the front (Fig. 21b). The structure can be differentiated from natural, lichen-covered stones by its lack of lichen. Grass grew inside the structure. The inner part of the rock shelter forms a light slope to the northwest. The structure has been disturbed by passing musk-oxen, which left traces of wool at a prominent part of the drip line (Fig. 21b: 1) and shifted the stones of the structure near the rock wall (see: C. Pasda 2001, 325).

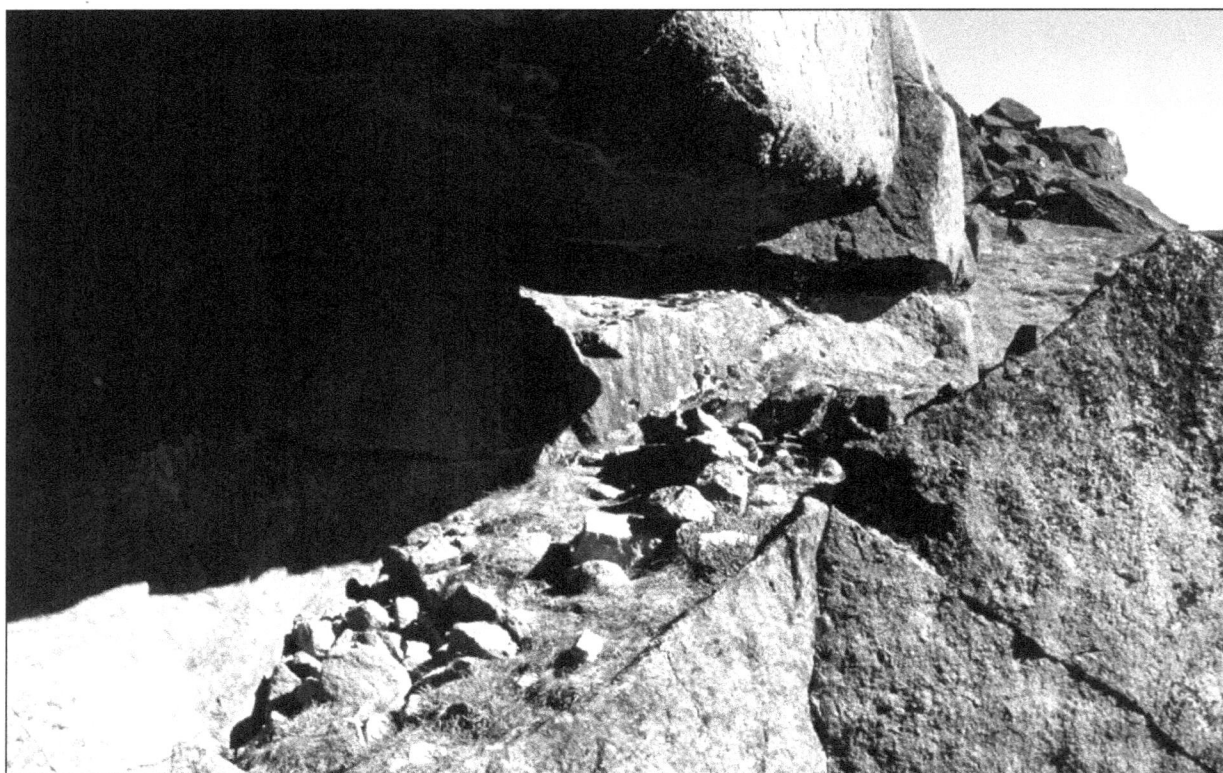

Fig. 21a: Resting and sleeping place in rock shelter (site FM 66V2-II-020) from west.

Another rock shelter is situated in approximately 1km distance as the crow flies. A large, rocky outcrop, some several tens of metres in extent, has a 2m deep but only 40cm high overhanging side exposed to the south. Under this overhang a rectangular structure was documented, with a wall, built out of stone and turf, at most 20cm high (Fig. 22). 3,5m away, in the ceiling of the overhang, is a nearly 1,8m deep, natural hole (Fig. 22: 1). Whether this hole points to an additional non-profane or non-functional use of the rock shelter remains speculative, but references found in literature and interviews (see chapter 3.1) show that such a role for this site is not impossible.

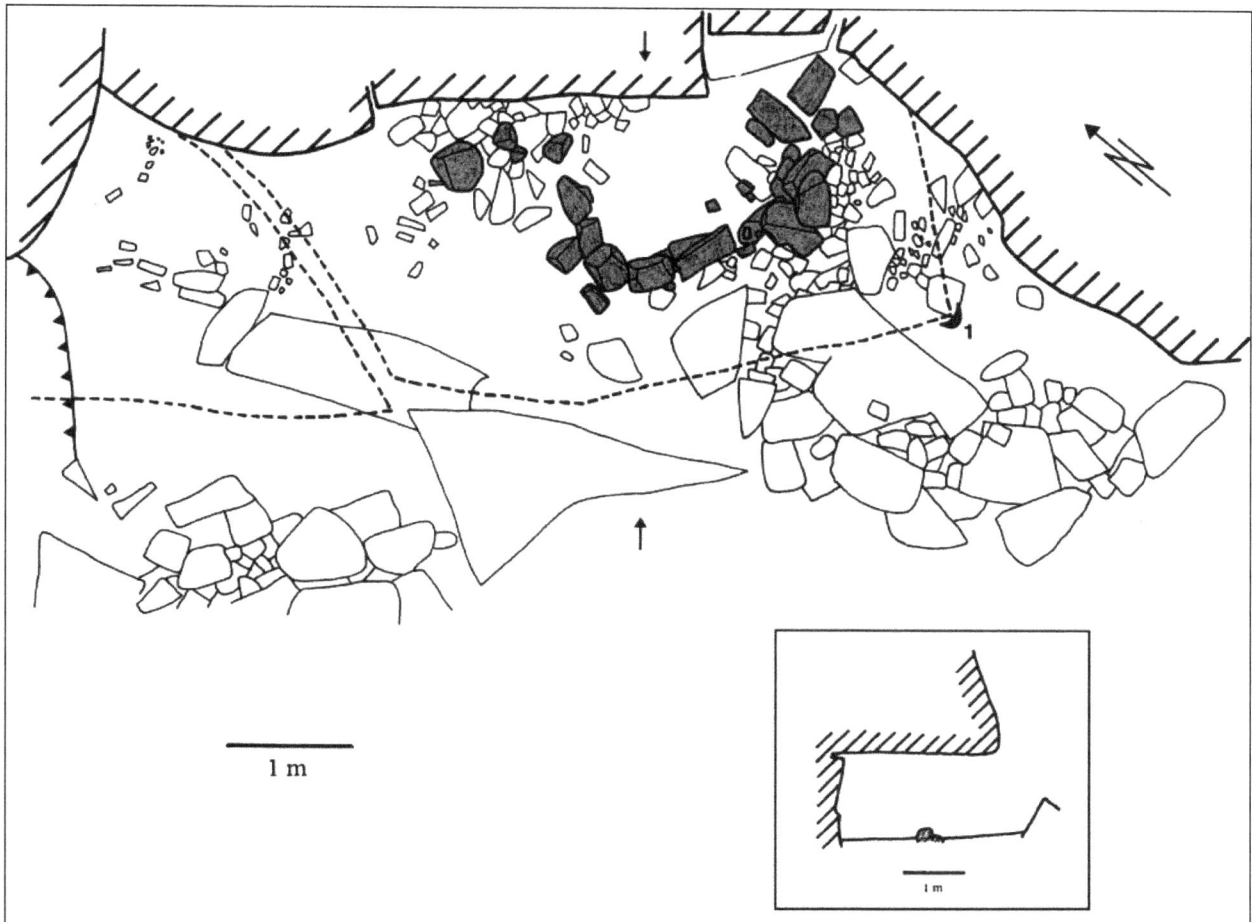

Fig. 21b: Resting and sleeping place in rock shelter (site FM 66V2-II-020) with musk-ox wool (1), rock wall (hatched), drip-line (broken line), archaeological structure (grey) and natural stones (white).

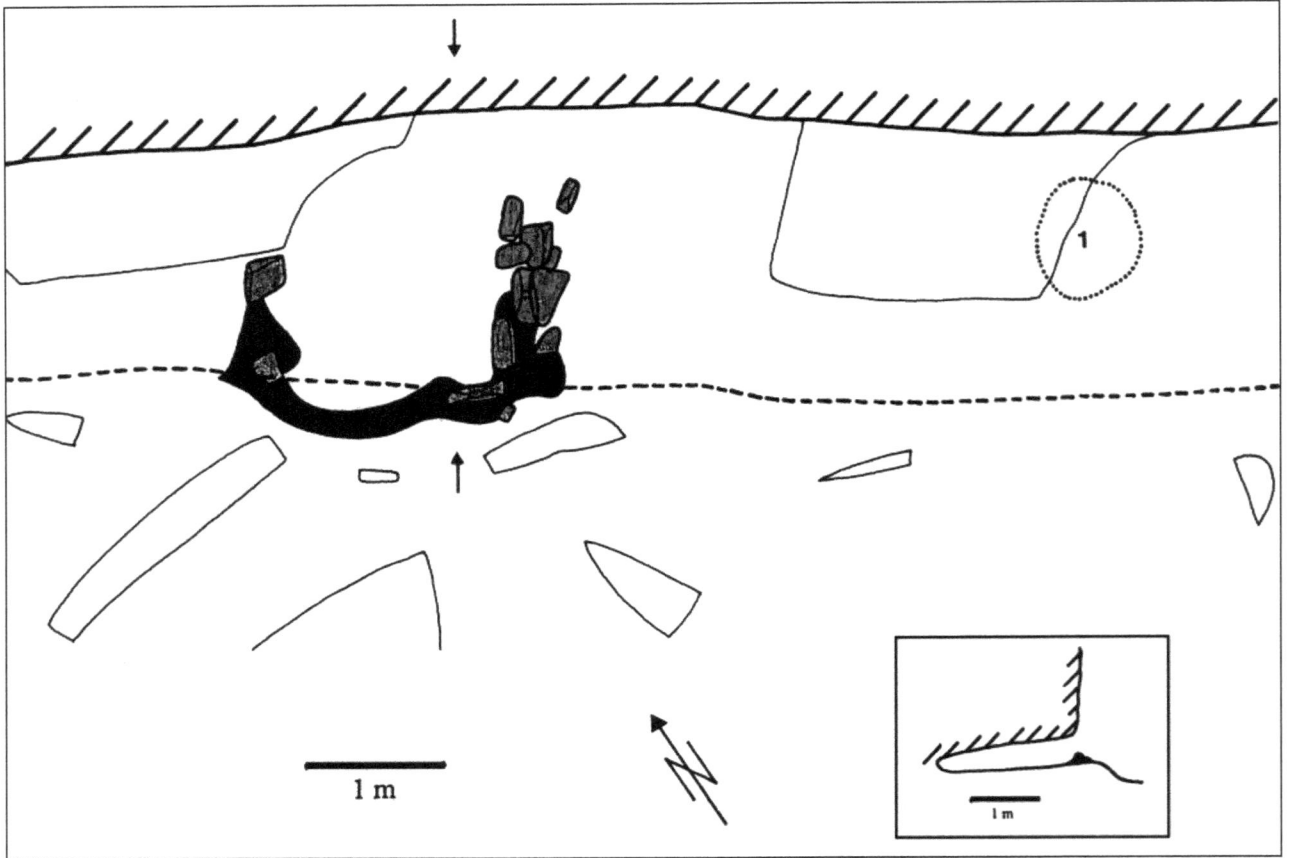

Fig. 22: Resting and sleeping place in rock shelter (site FM 66V2-II-034) with natural hollow in rock ceiling (1), rock wall (hatched), drip line (broken line), natural stones (white) and archaeological structure made out of stone (grey) and turf (black).

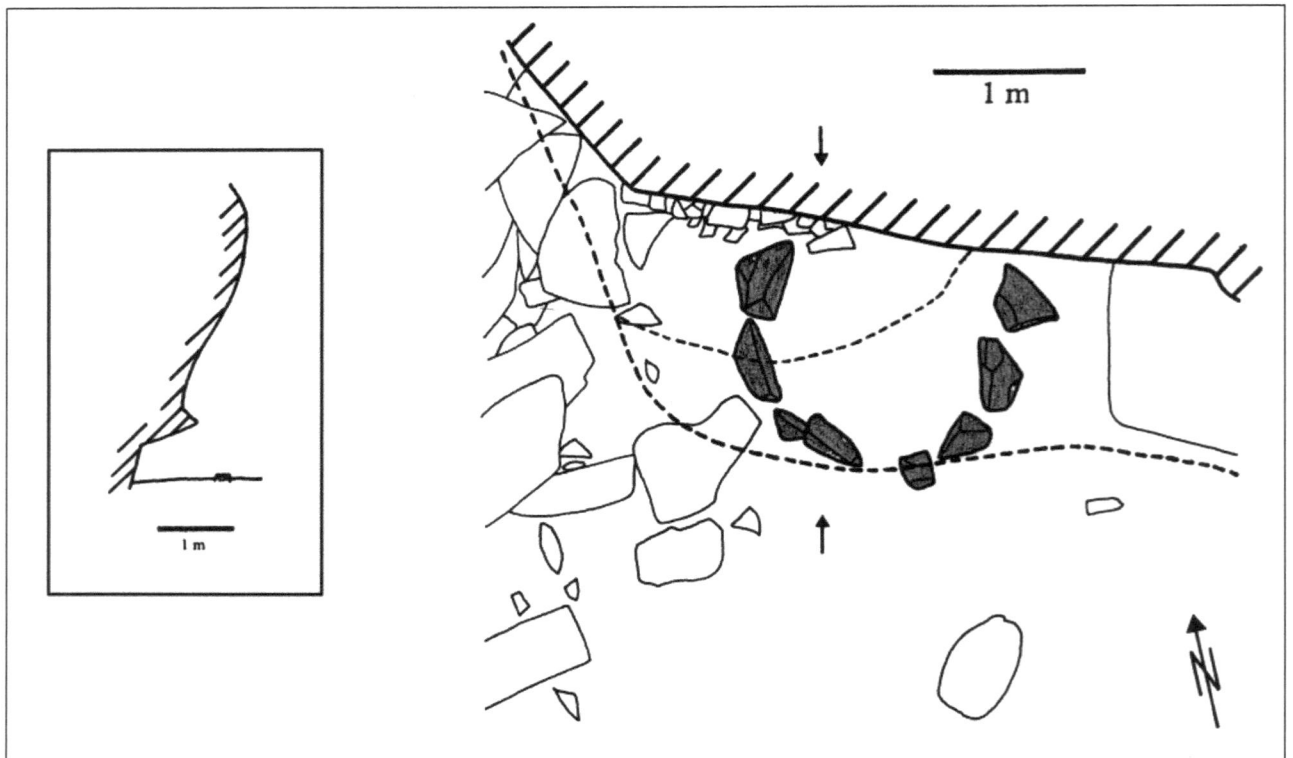

Fig. 23a: Resting and sleeping place in rock shelter (site FM 66V2-II-025). Illustration see fig. 22.

Fig. 23b: Resting and sleeping place in rock shelter (site FM 66V2-II-025) from east.

Another site was found 1-2km away from a large summer camp (Fig. 23). A circular structure was built out of few, today obliquely standing stones at the foot of a steep, slightly overhanging rock wall several tens of metres in height. The structure has a diameter of 1,5m and lies close to the back wall.

Approximately 3-4km away from another large summer camp a site was found with not a single, but several structures along a rock wall exposed to the southeast (Fig. 24a/b). Three structures were seen but only two are of unquestionably human origin. A structure built out of stones and turf can be seen not under but immediately outside the drip line of a 50cm high and 5m deep rock shelter (Fig. 24: 1). The stones are covered with lichen (Fig. 24c). The slightly distorted, at the present day oval-triangular form seems to be produced by slipping of stones and disintegration of turf-blocks. Inside the rock shelter several caribou bones were found. Another structure (Fig. 24: 3) built out of stone and turf (Fig. 24d) is situated approximately 20m to the northwest. Since bones are incorporated in the turf, this organic material seems to have been brought in as blocks of 70x30cm from the slope immediately below, where several further bones are situated in the sediments. The stones in the structure are not covered with lichen and are distributed in a more diffuse scatter. Several rib fragments, vertebrae, and sawn antler also occur. Two caribou antlers have been inserted by humans into a cleft in the rock wall above the structure (Fig. 24d). Antlers like these were only found in more recent sites (e.g. Fig. 26) and may have been used for hanging equipment or drying meat (pers. comm. B. Grønnow 7/25/2002).

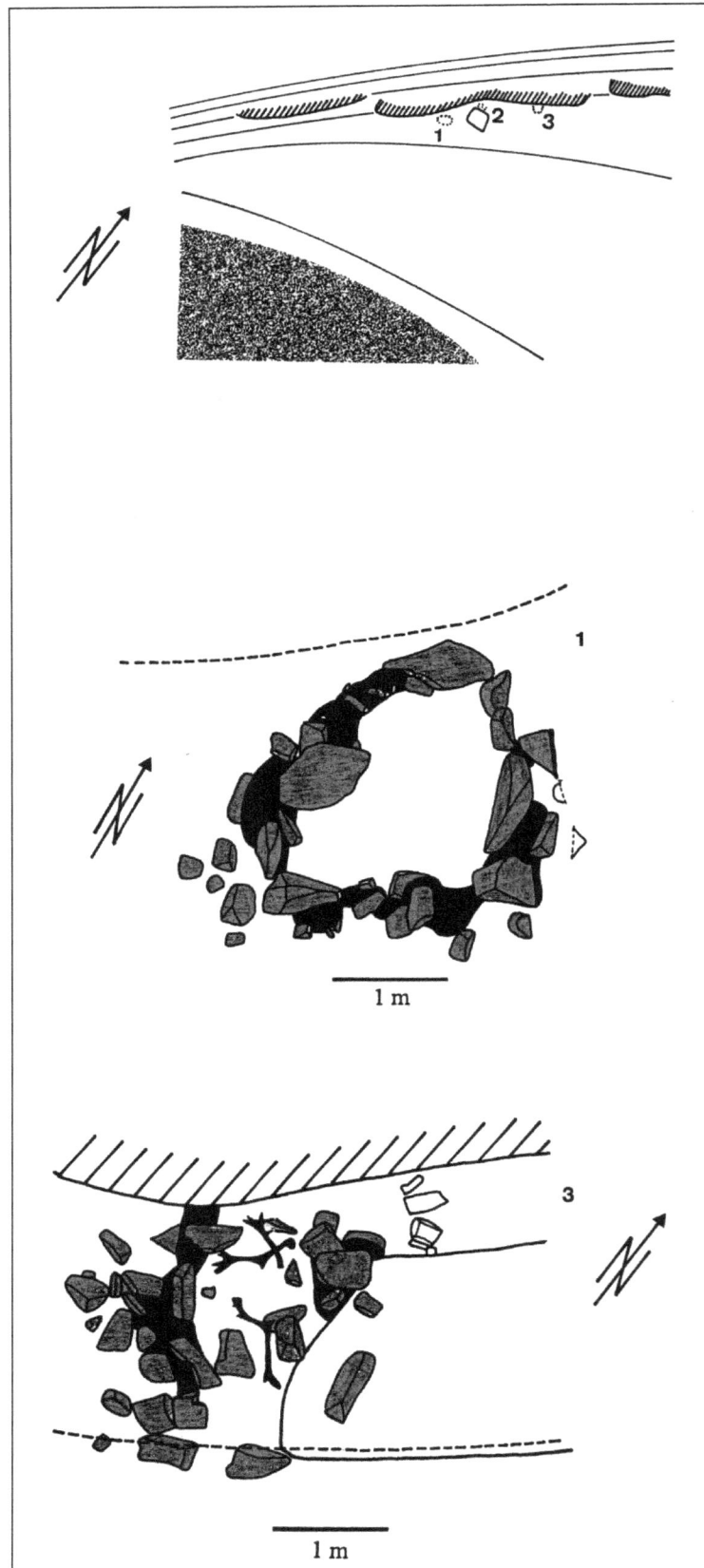

Fig. 24a: Rock wall with resting and sleeping places (site L609 in Odgaard et al. 2003) with sketch of topographical situation (above), lake (grey), rock wall (hatched), boulder (white), hunter's bed (1), used rock shelter (3). Illustration see fig. 22.

Fig. 24b: Rock wall with resting and sleeping places (site L609 in Odgaard et al. 2003) from east.

Fig. 24c: Hunters' bed 1 (site L609 in Odgaard et al. 2003) from east.

Fig. 24d: Used rock shelter 3 (site L609 in Odgaard et al. 2003) from southwest.

The next site is situated in the middle of an inland travel route, where five archaeological structures are situated over a distance of 70-80m (Fig. 25a: above) along a high rock wall (Fig. 25b). Only one structure is connected with a rock shelter: This one has a rectangular form of stones, today covered by lichen (Fig. 25: 1), in a niche between the rock wall and a boulder (Fig. 25c). Structure 2 and 3 are similar to structure 4, a rectangular turf wall with few stones (Fig. 25: 4), which are aligned against a large boulder in front of the rock wall. Located away from the rock wall and boulders, the last structure (Fig. 25a: 5) shows another form with its rounded wall built out of stones (Fig. 25d).

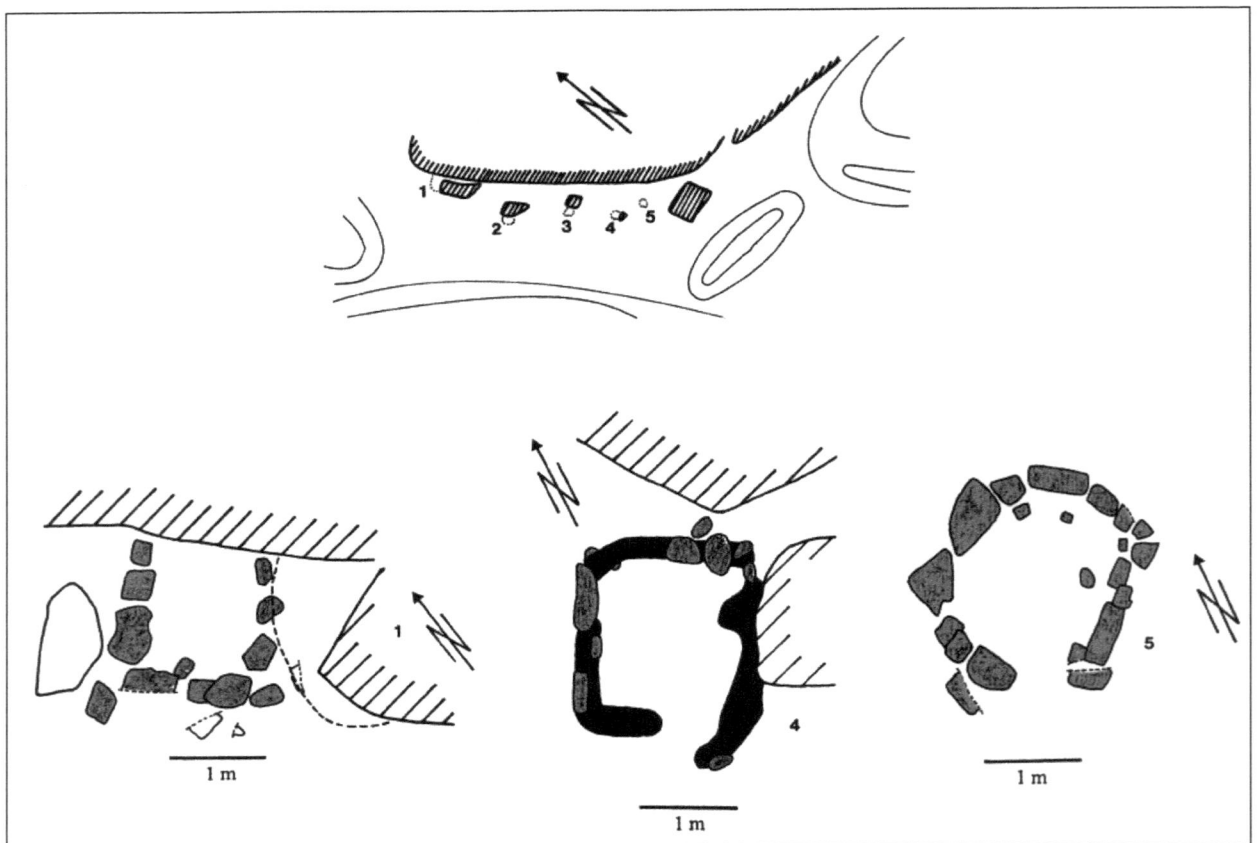

Fig. 25a: Rock wall with five resting and sleeping places (site FM 66V2-I-031) and sketch of topographical situation (above), used rock shelter (1), hunters' beds (2-5). Illustration see fig. 21 and 22.

Fig. 25b: Rock wall with five resting and sleeping places (site FM 66V2-I-031) from southwest.

Fig. 25c: Used rock shelter 1 (site FM 66V2-I-031) from northwest.

Fig. 25d: Hunters' bed 5 (site FM 66V2-I-031) from southwest.

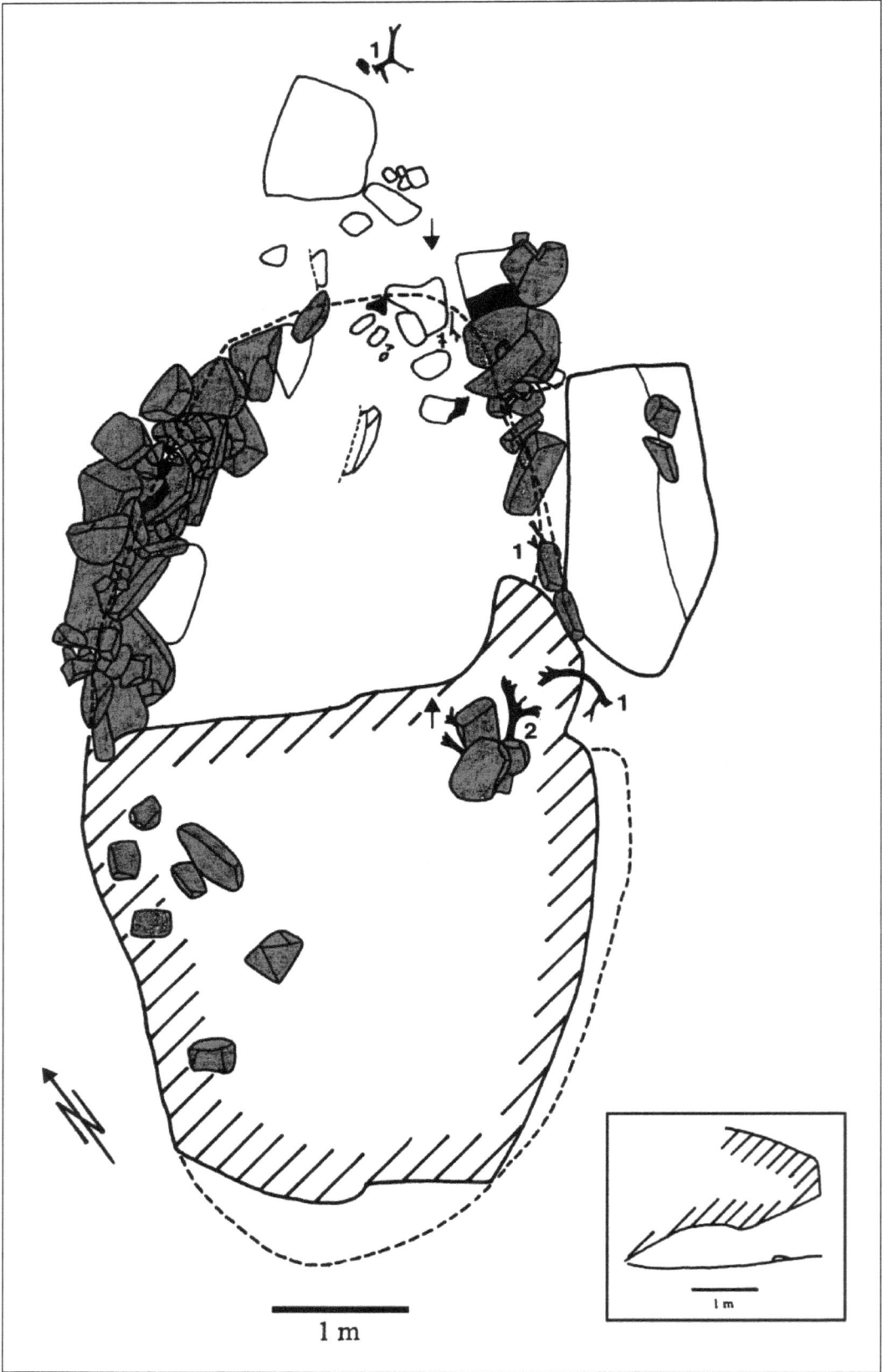

Fig. 26a: Resting and sleeping place in rock shelter (site L606 in Odgaard et al. 2003). Illustration see fig. 21 and 22

Fig. 26b: Resting and sleeping place in rock shelter (site L606 in Odgaard et al. 2003) from north.

Fig. 26c: Resting and sleeping place in rock shelter (site L606 in Odgaard et al. 2003) from northwest.

Fig. 26d: Wall from resting and sleeping place in rock shelter (site 606 in Odgaard et al. 2003) from northwest.

Fig. 26e: Resting and sleeping place in rock shelter (site L606 in Odgaard et al. 2003) from southeast.

The sites presented until now are rather simple structures, with walls built out of stones and/or turf, but in research area 2 more complex situations have been found. At a height of approximately 135m above the summer camp Qornoq kitdleq at Lake Tasersiaq is situated a large boulder with overhanging sides to the north and south (Fig. 27). Under the southern side can be seen a massive, semi-circular wall built out of several stones (Fig. 27a: 1; 27b). Some stones are covered with lichen, while others are not (Fig. 27b) and moss is present between them. Some deposits are built out of large stone slabs (Fig. 27a: 2), some use small natural hollows between boulders under the overhang (Fig. 27a: 4, 5; 27c). Large slabs to the north (Fig. 27a: 3) may be remnants of a former stone wall which was rebuilt into a small repository. In front of the structure several caribou bones were seen, but only one bone (which was taken for absolute dating) was documented in its original position (Fig. 27a: 6). Nearby, two fragments of wooden shafts were found (Fig. 27a: 7, 8). If these have been parts of arrows this locality may have been used before AD 1810 (Grønnow/Meldgaard/Nielsen 1983, 27). However, in the summer camp Qornoq kitdleq, below this rock shelter, parts of a kayak with metal nails have been found, which in West Greenland point to boats not more than 100 years old (H.C. Petersen 1986b, 26). As the rock shelter is situated at the most easiest access route to the summer camp this naturally confined locality may have been used during two centuries at least.

At only one point in research area 2 was a structure discovered which had been built with a large expenditure of effort. This site is situated in an isolated location on a plateau approximately 700m above the Paradise Valley some 7km as the crow flies from the large summer camp Eqalummiut aasivii (Grønnow 1986, 72) in the same valley. A large boulder, very exposed to the wind, has, on its northeastern side, a 3m deep and 60cm high cave-like overhang (Fig. 26a). Two sides were closed with stones so that only a 1,5m wide entrance is left open (Fig. 26b). As the side exposed to the southeast is protected by a natural boulder (Fig. 26e) only a few stones were used to close that side, whereas the side exposed to the northwest was carefully closed with several stones (Fig. 26c, d). On top of the boulder an antler is situated which is fixed by several stones (Fig. 26a: 2; 26b). Under the drip line is found grass with musk-ox-wool. In contrast to the structures shown before this site was built with a lot of expenditure of effort: The stones and up to 50cm long slabs had to be carried over several hundred metres, maybe by several persons together, and the open space between these stones had to be filled with small pebbles and moss (Fig. 26a: black). Striking is the strong lichen cover on the large stones of the wall, whereas smaller stones seem to be more lichen-free (Fig. 26d). This might result out of repeated maintenance and repair of the wall and could point to a long term use of the site. This interpretation might be supported by two concentrations outside, one of heavy weathered caribou bones and antlers alongside the other with almost fresh and sawed bones and antlers (K. Pasda in prep.). The last use of the structure seems to have been in modern times, as shown by parts of a rope, two matches and one cartridge *Norma 55*.

Another site is situated one day's march away from the next large summer camp. This site shows that boulders isolated in the landscape (Fig. 28a) were used as focal points to erect tents (Fig. 28c) and tent-house-like structures (Fig. 28b, d, e). The latter, built to be used as a house for many weeks, have possibly been re-used and rebuilt into hunters' beds.

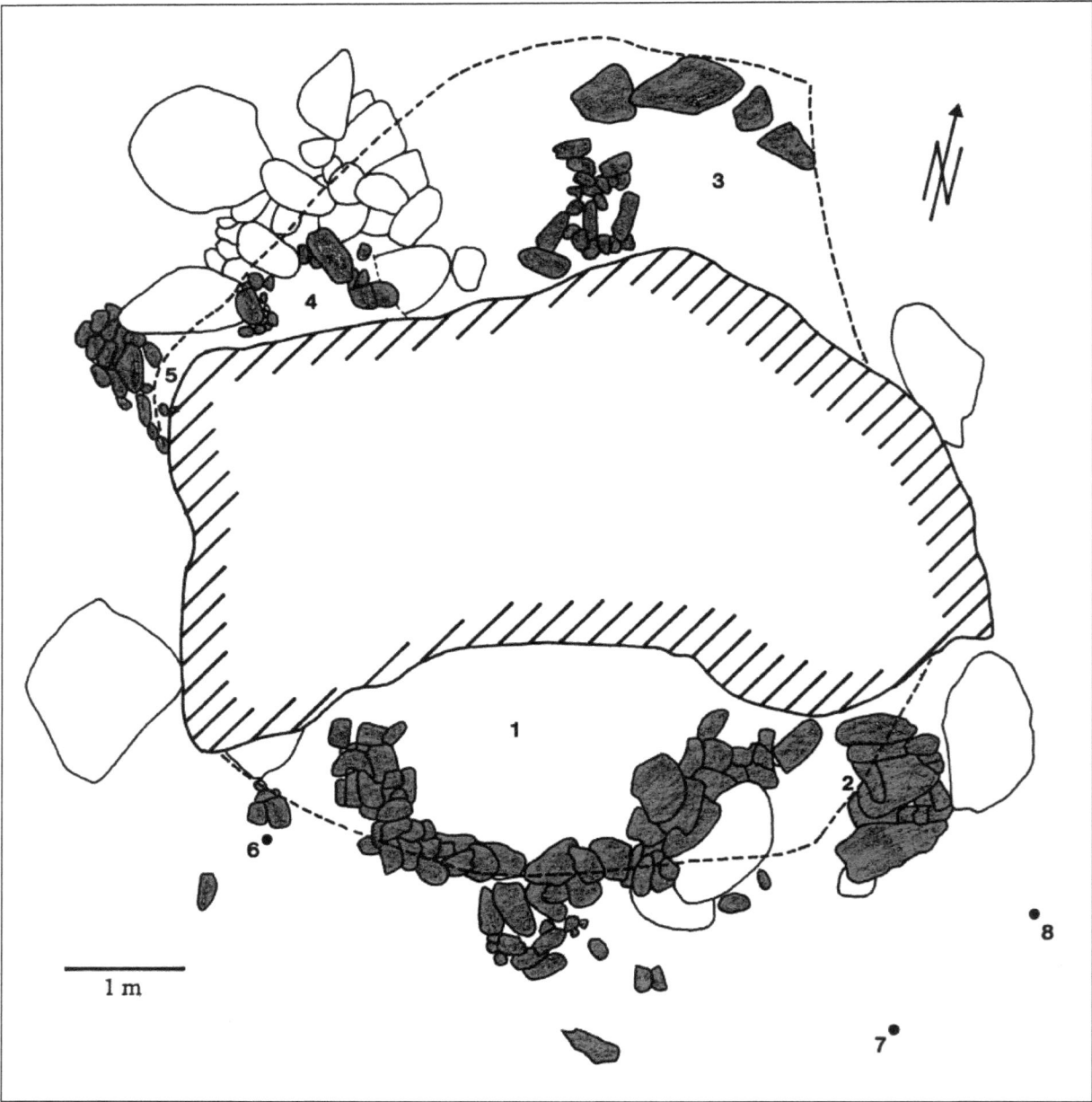

Fig. 27a: Boulder (site L620 in Odgaard et al. 2003) with resting and sleeping place (1), deposits (2-5), bone (6) and wooden arrow-shafts (7, 8). Illustration see Fig. 21 and 22.

Fig. 27b: Boulder (site L620 in Odgaard et al. 2003) with resting and sleeping place from east.

Fig. 27c: Boulder (site L620 in Odgaard et al. 2003) with deposit 4 from west.

Fig. 28a: Boulder (site FM 66V2-II-011) with natural shaled stone slab and archaeological structures from southeast.

Fig. 28b: Boulder (site FM 66V2-II-011) with tent-house-like structure from southeast.

Fig. 28c: Stone slab from boulder (site FM 66V2-II-011) with tent ring from northeast.

Fig. 28d: Boulder (site FM 66V2-II-011) with second tent-house-like structure from north.

Fig. 28e: Boulder (site FM 66V2-II-011) with second tent-house-like structure from southeast.

A rock shelter surrounded by several other structures is situated on a spur of land with a large boulder (Fig. 29a: 1). Bone refuse (K. Pasda in prep.) is scattered on the slope to the east and between the boulder (Fig. 29a: 1) and the hunters' bed (Fig. 29a: 6). At the overhanging eastern side of the boulder a stone wall (Fig. 29a: 2) built out of long stones (Fig. 29b) measuring up to 80cm protects an area of some 2x2m. Some stones are now lying at the front, 2m down the slope. As the stone wall is made out of both lichen-covered and lichen-free stones a long use and frequent rebuilding of the structure can be assumed. The lichen-cover of the stones of the deposit (Fig. 29a: 3) with caribou bones looks similar. Under the small overhanging, triangular south-western edge is situated an unclear structure (Fig. 29a: 5) made out of head-sized stones. Maybe this is a lightly built protection against the wind. In the open, away and below the boulder, a 4x2m large hunters' bed can be seen, made out of 20-40cm long stones, which are partly covered with lichen and overgrown by turf and grass (Fig. 29a: 6). Between caribou paths in a small pass-like situation below the boulder are two rounded, 1m long and 20-50cm deep shooting-coverts made out of head-sized stones, today covered by lichen (Fig. 29a: 7, 8). Further south a head-sized *inussuk* is situated on a large natural boulder (Fig. 29a: 9).

Even at large summer camps stone walls were built in useful cave-like situations. On one site a used 2-3m wide cleft between two boulders (Fig. 30) is surrounded by several tent-houses. The stone wall is made out of stone slabs which have later fallen to the inside and outside (Fig. 30b, c). Maybe this was done by musk-oxen whose wool could be seen everywhere. Occupation of musk-oxen inside may also have resulted in movement of material remains to the inner sides of the rock walls. Bones found in the cave were a caribou rib and calcaneum, a seal mandible (Fig. 30a: 2), a second rib from caribou and a proximal human humerus (Fig. 30a: 3). Around a large piece of turf (Fig. 30a: 1) were ribs and long bone fragments of caribou, under the drip line (Fig. 30a: 5) were fragments of mandibles, small antlers, ribs and long bones of caribou. Only one antler was situated below a shifted stone slab in the centre of the cleft (Fig. 30a: 4). Turf was incorporated in the stone wall (Fig. 30a: black). Large pieces of turf with bones were also lying inside (Fig. 30a: 1). Maybe they were brought in from the tent-houses in the vicinity. Therefore the single bones inside may be brought in incorporated in turf too. Or the bones are a product of natural activities, e.g. by polar fox (K. Pasda 2001). The human bone may derive from the direct surroundings too, where at least one grave is situated. Whether this bone was brought in by humans or animals cannot be decided. The closest source for seal is the fjord Kangerlussuaq, that means 10km away and 640m below the site. In the same area, at another site with three tent-rings and one rock shelter in the Paradise Valley, situated 10-15km from the fjord, several seal bones have been found and were interpreted by Grønnow (1986, 79) as provisions used while travelling inland. The same can be seen at Aasivissuit where seal bones represent remains of provisions carried to the camp (Grønnow/Meldgaard/Nielsen 1983, 69-70). The occurrence of a single seal mandible is striking as it does not bear that much meat. But in general bone occurrence at sites seems to be influenced more by differential transport and utilization by humans, caching, dog feeding and natural post-depositional processes (Lyman/Savelle/Whitridge 1992). Also of interest for this study is an observation made during the rainy field-season in 2002: After 11 hours of rain and drizzle this particular rock shelter was so wet due to water dripping inside that to use this natural confined locality for protection against rain is impossible.

Fig. 29a: Boulder (site FM 66V2-II-016) with resting and sleeping place (2), deposit (3), polar fox den (4), triangular structure (5), hunters' bed (6), shooting-coverts (7, 8), inussuit (9) and caribou pathes (grey).

Fig. 29b: Boulder (site FM 66V2-II-016) with resting and sleeping place 2 from northeast.

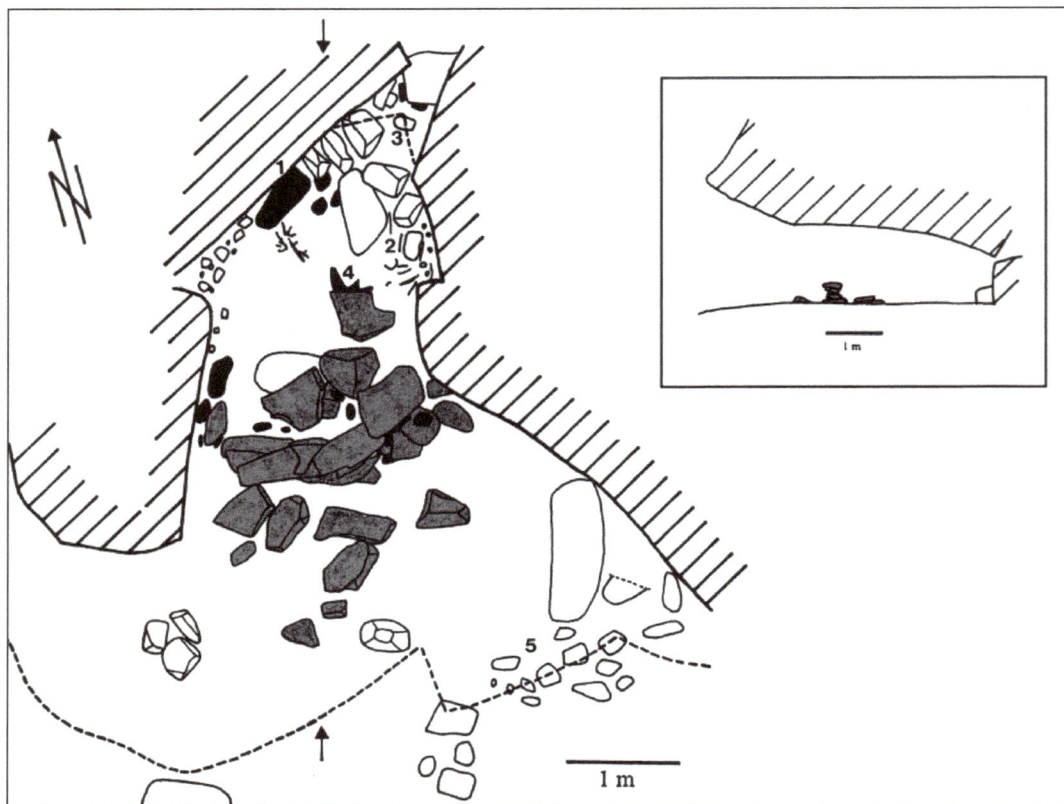

Fig. 30a: Resting and sleeping place in rock shelter (site L505 in Odgaard et al. 2003). Illustration see fig. 21.

Fig. 30b: Resting and sleeping place under boulder (site L505 in Odgaard et al. 2003) from south.

Fig. 30c: Inner part of resting and sleeping place under boulder (site L505 in Odgaard et al. 2003) from south.

Unquestionable evidence of fastening of a tent roof to rock walls, boulders or rock shelters could not be found in the research area. To the description of overnight-stays in rock shelters by Gripp (1941/42, 43-44) given above, it must be added that the tent roof was a ground sheet of the geologists borrowed and used by the Greenlanders. The remains of tent-houses and tent-rings close to stone walls (Fig. 16) do not speak against fastening skin or cloth. Further hints can be seen in simple linear rows of single stones on the ground in front of overhanging boulders (Fig. 31). Maybe here a tent wall was fixed on the ground. In contrast single stones on large boulders (e.g. Fig. 28a-c) may have been put there to fix the tent roof.

Fig. 31: Single stones in row under drip line of rock shelter (site L531 in Odgaard et al. 2003).

Striking is the fact that nearly every rock shelter site with an archaeological structure yields either no or only few tools. Artefacts from the historic period were only found once: The two arrow shaft fragments in the site above the summer camp Qornoq kitdleq (Fig. 27). Other artefacts were found at recent sites, in the repository at Aasivissuit (Fig. 9) and around the isolated, cave-like rock shelter on the plateau (Fig. 26). However, the lack of artefacts on open-air sites is a characteristic of the research area. This may be connected with short stays just during the warm season (e.g. Hehmsoth-LeMouël 1999, 82) combined with no or few activities leaving artefacts on the surface (Grønnow/Meldgaard/Nielsen 1983, 53). But natural processes can be responsible too, since strong and rapid vegetation growth in low lying areas (e.g. Kramer 1996, 41-42; Schilling 1996, 115-116) make artefacts invisible while slow vegetation growth and slow soil development in higher areas (Grønnow 1986, 67) may destroy artefacts. Field-observation on recent, historic and prehistoric sites in 2001-2002 and taphonomic investigations on caribou bones (K. Pasda 2001) may show that organic remains can be more or less completely destroyed by weathering after approximately 100 years.

Waste areas were seen just on two sites (Fig. 26; 29) where several square-metres large bone scatters covered the slopes in front of the rock shelter (K. Pasda in press). On one single rock shelter of all sites seen in 1999-2003 a dense dump area was discovered (Fig. 32). On one side of a large boulder several hundred animal bones covered the surface under the overhang. The boulder is situated in the centre of a large summer camp with several tent-houses. Due to long snow cover on the northern side of the boulder (Photos by S. Malmqvist) preservation of bones is exceptional. With this site it seems as if dealing with waste is different in rock shelters with rare refuse scatters outside, in contrast to summer camps with distinct dump areas.

Fig. 32a: Concentration of bones and antlers under east side of the overhanging boulder at the summer camp Qornoq kangigdleq (site L563 in Odgaard et al. 2003) from north.

Fig. 32b: Concentration of bones and antlers under north side of the overhanging boulder at the summer camp Qornoq kangigdleq (site L563 in Odgaard et al. 2003) from north.

Fig. 32c: Detail of the concentration of bones and antlers under north side of the overhanging boulder (site L563 in Odgaard et al. 2003) from north.

In each rock shelter and under each overhanging boulder were found tracks and dung of songbirds, grouse, snow hare, polar fox, caribou and musk-ox. These animals bring in food particles and nesting material and cause characteristic changes in surface sediments (C. Pasda 2001). However, archaeological structures are disturbed by animals larger than polar fox, such as caribou and musk-ox. The latter is not a natural component of the fauna of the research area, since some musk-ox from High Arctic areas were released here approximately 40 years ago (Olesen 1991). Musk-oxen were often observed near boulders (Pedersen 1936, 39, 65), a habit which can be demonstrated by their wool left at such locations (e.g. Fig. 13: 1; 19: 1; 21b: 1). As, in the research area, male musk-ox have an average weight of approximately 300kg (Olesen/Thing/Aastrup 1994), the movement of even the large rocks of stone walls is feasible. This results in simple downward movements (Fig. 27a: 1; 29a: 2), disconnecting parts near the back of the rock shelter (Fig. 21), movement of stones to the inside and outside (Fig. 30) as well as nearly the almost complete destruction of a structure (Fig. 24a: 3).

The anthropogenic character of single structures found is rarely as clear as for those described above. Between the two rock shelter sites documented in fig. 19 and 22 was documented an indistinct, more or less rectangular structure of turf and stones (Fig. 33). Striking were the occurrence of stones directly under different drip-lines or steps in the stone roof above the structure (drawn in fig. 33a with differently hatched lines). A stone (Fig. 33a: narrow hatching) with a freshly broken surface lying on a large slab at the southeast edge of the structure (Fig. 33b: in foreground) resembled loose stones in a cleft in the back rock wall 2m above. Whether this is an argument for a natural formation of the whole structure due to stones fallen from different drip-lines on to the surface and subsequent local overgrowth of them with turf, cannot be decided with certainty. To add a remark, three years after field-work the author is also sceptic about the anthropogenic origin of the two stones in the rock shelter documented in Fig. 20. However, structures due to natural phenomena like debris slides, micro-mudflows, hydrostatic effects of water, wind erosion, solifluction or slump, as described by Everett (1967) from research area 2, were not found in rock shelters. Only a movement of stones due to weathering of turf and sod parts between stones was observed (e.g. Fig. 24a: 1).

The results show that, in the vicinity of regularly used areas, localities and travel routes in the landscape, nearly all rock walls, boulders and rock shelters have been used in the different ways shown in chapter 3.1. Maybe spatial size determines the function of natural confined localities. However, the most important reason whether they are used or not and how they are used seems to lie in their relationship to other sites and therefore in their position in the cultural landscape. The exact number of used rock shelters in a landscape depends on different methodological problems; e.g. whether one counts all structures found in a region or just the number of sites, or whether one considers only the resting and sleeping places or all the possibilities of using boulders mentioned in chapter 3.1. Altogether, the low number of rock shelter sites in the inland of West Greenland has to be emphasized: Pind et al. (1991, 83) found 147 sites in research area 1, among them three rock shelters used as sleeping places. This figure was confirmed by our two year-survey in 1999 and 2000 in the same area which was focused on looking behind every boulder attractive for human occupation. In the Nuuk area Gulløv (1983, 187-198) reports 21 caves with archaeological records among 429 sites. In the northwestern part of research area 2 Grønnow (1986, Tab. 1) found 40 sites with 155 structures, among them four rock shelters with archaeological finds. In research area 2 approximately 10% of all sites found in 2001 (Gabriel et al. 2002) and approximately 5% of all sites found in 2002 (Odgaard et al. 2003) are used rock shelters. These numbers show that in the inland of West Greenland not more than one tenth of all archaeological sites are represented by rock shelters. Maybe regions with a large hinterland far away from main fjords and primary access routes, such as research area 2, have more (~10%) rock shelters whereas hunting in areas with fast access from fjords and summer camps, such as research area 1, did not depend that much on naturally confined sites, resulting in a low percentage (<5%) of used rock shelters.

Fig. 33a: Dubious archaeological structure in rock shelter (site FM 66V2-II-033). Illustration see Fig. 21-23.

Fig. 33b: Dubious archaeological structure in rock shelter (site FM 66V2-II-033) from east.

In summary, the following can be said about the results from eleven rock shelter sites documented in detail (Fig. 19-27; 29; 30) from the inland region of Central West Greenland. The area protected by a natural overhang is small and does not exceed 10m². The used area, defined as the area protected by a built structure, is smaller with an average of 3,5m² and does not exceed the space in communal winter houses at the coast where each person had an average of 1,1-3,8m² (Lee/Reinhardt 2003, 173). The value of 3,5m² is indeed probably too high, since the two largest rock shelters are taken into consideration. Here a large, cave-like natural confined area needed to be secured by just by a frontal (Fig. 30) or two lateral walls (Fig. 26) and without these two sites a protected area of around 2,7m² would be the most typical for the research area. This small protected space has to be seen against the background of the much smaller body-size of Neo-Eskimo humans compared to modern citizens of West Greenland (Jørgensen 1989): In the Thule culture the average body height of men was around 160cm, of women around 150cm (e.g. Fischer-Møller 1938), increasing in colonial times (e.g. Hansen 1893).

The archaeological structures occur under slightly overhanging high rock walls (4 cases) and in niches between boulders (1 case) as well as under low (1-1,4m) overhangs (4 cases). However, very low (~50cm) rock shelters, just penetrable by crawling on all fours, have also been used (2 cases).

Possibly only those localities were used which have conditions particular favourable for humans. Most used rock shelters had a south-western (4 cases) or southern (3 cases) exposure. Exposure to the southeast (2 cases) and west (1 case) is rare. The boulder on the plateau (Fig. 26) with heavily constructed walls is the only recorded example of an entrance with northern exposure. Here other features, such as proximity to a plateau suitable for hunting and the only natural protection in this area made this locality an attractive place frequently used by hunters.

All used rock shelters were situated near running water. Proximity to running water was not important for only two sites (Fig. 26; 27) which are located several minutes march away from a creek or lake.

The amount of work invested for constructing structures ranges from placement of two stones (1 case) to building strong walls out of more than 300 stones (3 cases). However, walls were most commonly built out of approximately 10-30 stones (7 cases). The youngest sites, used until short time ago (Fig. 24a: 3; 26; 30), show that turf, sod and moss also have been used. This organic material may have been weathered away at the older structures (see e.g. Fig. 23; 25a: 1), but the use of stones by themselves seems feasible when rock shelters are situated far away from areas with turf, sod or moss (e.g. Fig. 21).

The form of the walls is mainly rectangular, sometimes with rounded edges (7 cases). However, semi-circular forms (1 case) and one site with just two stones (1 case) are also found. In two rock shelters the form and position of the wall is defined by the natural overhang, giving frontal (Fig. 30) or lateral (Fig. 26) constructions.

The lack of tools has been discussed above. A few bones occurred at some sites inside, but it is not that clear if these bones are remains of human consumption or a product of carnivore activity (e.g. Fig. 30). In contrast to previous archaeological surveys and ethnographic sources fireplaces were not found. Maybe meat and fat were grilled on flat stones heated with burnt heather (R. Petersen 2003, 39). Then the flat stones in some rock shelters (Fig. 27a: 2) can represent fireplaces, maybe later re-used as deposits (Fig. 29a: 3).

Exact dating of the sites is difficult. Ethnographic sources, form and preservation of structures, lichen cover and the preservation of bones suggest that all sites are of Neo-Eskimo origin. This means that the sites documented here have been built and used in Thule, historic and recent times (Møbjerg 1998, 99-100) and – according to a ^{14}C-date (Odgaard et al. 2003) on bones from a summer camp of the Thule culture (Fig. 16b) - may not be more than 700 years old.

The differences of lichen cover on the stones of a wall and the occurrence at a site of bones showing different weathering stages might be interpreted as showing successive use over many decades, even centuries, implying repair and maintenance of structures. If structures were not changed but just maintained, the use and function of rock shelter sites remained the same over decades or centuries. If this is true, the interpretation suggested in chapter 2, that the use of rock shelters is not affected by changing settlement patterns, would be supported by archaeological evidence. This result of research shows some consequences for the interpretation of human lifestyle which would develop out of archaeological work focused on caves and rock shelters alone: In the Central West Greenlandic interior a concentration on cave and rock shelter archaeology would point to a stereotype of highly mobile, small hunting groups which used the interior regularly in an unchanging manner over centuries. That means that in the research area, without excavations, changes of settlement patterns can only be seen in open-air sites. Then the creation of landscape drawn out through time by people who moved in it and their meanings and perceptions of place (Barrett 1999, 24) may be investigated the best in open-air sites.

Tab. 2: Characteristics of used rock shelters in the inland of Central West Greenland

-natural protected space:	Small
-used space:	very small
-finds:	almost none (very rarely tools, few bones)
-built structures:	rectangular and oval walls built out of stones and/or turf
-amount of work:	some minutes/hours
-maintenance:	partly, sometimes intensive
-re-use:	partly, then successive over a longer period
-change of function:	None
-waste areas:	rarely (if present: bone scatters outside)
-function:	resting place or overnight stay (protection against wind and cold, conserving body heat) during travels or hunting expeditions

To summarize (Tab. 2), rock shelters have been used as resting places and for overnight stays in summer while travelling inland from the coast and fjords and back, as well as during hunting expeditions in the hinterland of the main hunting areas. Rock shelters provided shelter against cold and wind, partly against rain. Built structures provide additional support against cold and wind and are therefore very small. This demonstrates the use of rock shelters by only a few persons. The reason for the small and protected space used by several individuals in rock shelters, which is smaller than average space for one individual in winter houses, is to conserve body heat. As these places have been used by only a few persons with little equipment for some hours only not much waste producing activity can be expected – with the exception of consumption of food. The latter occurred rarely and resulted in waste areas outside where on the slope in front of rock shelters bone scatters are visible. As can be seen by the maintenance of walls without changing their structure, rock shelters may have been used successively without a change in their function. This shows that the use of rock shelters in the interior of Central West Greenland was generally the same as by hunter-gatherers worldwide (Galanidou 2000), where mainly small rock shelters were used with rare alteration of the protected space and only a few objects which could survive weathering being abandoned.

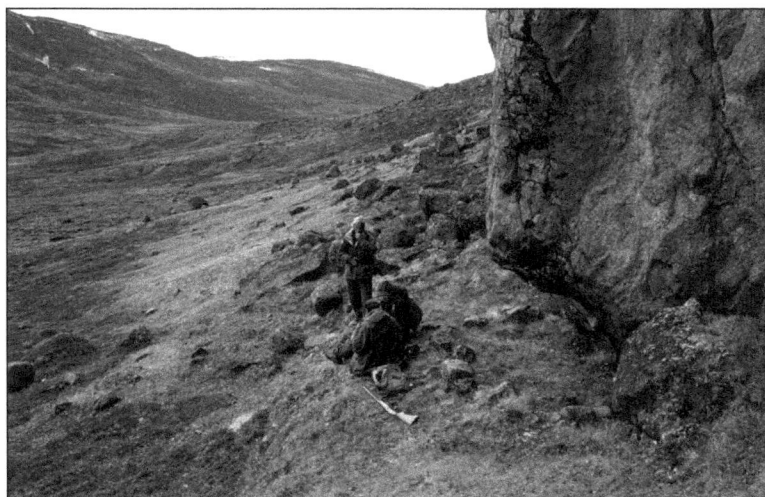

Fig. 34a: Comparison of resting and sleeping places: used rock shelter (site FM 66V2-II-041).

Fig. 34b: Comparison of resting and sleeping places: hunters' bed (site L557 in Odgaard et al. 2003).

Fig. 34c: Comparison of resting and sleeping places: hunters' bed (site L560 in Odgaard et al. 2003).

The structures in rock shelters may have had the same function as the hunters' beds; both occur in the same areas more or less in the same numbers (Fig. 3), even together at one site (Fig. 24; 25; 29). As described in chapter 2, both have been used in the same way over centuries as resting and sleeping places during minor caribou-hunting expeditions. The built structures of both rock shelters (Fig. 34a) and hunters' beds (Fig. 34b, c) are similar in form, size and construction. Fireplaces are rarely found at resting and sleeping places in the open and under rock shelters. If present, fireplaces are situated not in but beside a hunters' bed (Grønnow/Meldgaard/Nielsen 1983, Fig. 10). No fireplaces have been found inside stone walls in rock shelters. If the flat stones in used rock shelters (Fig. 27a: 2; 29a: 3) indicate fireplaces, then fireplaces in naturally confined localities also occur outside the built structure. As seen in the research area, the construction patterns of hunters' beds have rarely been changed by its human users. Therefore the function of hunters´ beds remained stable over a long time span. These common characteristics show that when a small number of mobile caribou-hunters used resting and sleeping places in West Greenland the archaeological record left behind is the same at naturally confined localities (=used rock shelters) and at open-air sites (=hunters' beds). This interpretation could confirm a result of the synthesis by Galanidou (2000, 266, 272) that, in general, the use of caves and open-air sites is more or less similar within one group of a society/culture but varies between different groups. For example, in the interior of Central West Greenland fireplaces are not situated in but beside the sleeping area: As described above, beside used rock shelters and beside hunters' beds as well as in the entrance of tent-houses (Grønnow/Meldgaard/Nielsen 1983, 26-27). This implies that the nature and appearance of structures and the spatial distribution of objects and refuse are a culturally specific phenomenon (Galanidou 2000, 251, 253, 255, 270) and result out of how people of a particular culture perceive and organize space, how they consume and behave at a place, and of how they estimate comfort, cleanness and security: Just as architecture presupposes sense, presentation, planning, construction and maintenance of a built structure, so there exist certain elements of the spatial organisation of a specific culture which are independent of the natural setting.

4. Conclusions

According to Gamble (2001, 15) *"archaeology is basically about three things: objects, landscapes and what we make of them"*. The investigation presented here is about rock shelter sites used by arctic hunter-gatherers. The physical landscape is the tundra of continental climate in the interior of Central West Greenland which was investigated by field-surveys from 1999-2002. The humanised landscape of Angujaartorfiup Nunaa and the region between the upper Kangerlussuaq and Isortoq was created by prehistoric, historic and recent Greenlanders who came inland to hunt caribou in summer.

In the research area archaeologist Bjarne Grønnow has combined archaeological evidence with ethno-historic information in order to interpret the use of caves and rock shelters: Natural confined localities were used during caribou-hunting in summer as resting and sleeping places by few individuals or small groups during brief stays while travelling inland and back, as well as on minor hunting expeditions in the far hinterland.

According to ethno-historic sources walls of stone and turf were built in rock shelters to protect a narrow space with just enough place for some individuals to crawl in. People slept in their clothes on the floor which was filled with heather and twigs. The construction served as a protection to preserve body heat. The equipment of human users of rock shelters is reduced to the most necessary. The archaeological evidence of this behaviour is represented by small rectangular and oval walls built out of stone and turf with rare fireplaces outside the structure and rare waste areas of bone refuse outside the rock shelter.

In addition, a review of the ethnographic and ethno-historic sources shows the large variability in using caves, rock shelters and boulders: They were used as shooting-coverts, hunting-stands, deposits, repositories, meat caches or as marker-points which were maintained and upgraded. Naturally confined localities were used as resting and sleeping places during travels in winter and summer in the inland and at the coast, as fox-traps, graves, offering site or to support the cover of tents and tent-houses.

But caves, rock shelters and boulders were also perceived as important sites without material record left by humans: As a place to meet for telling stories, as a locality were mythical beings live, as an opening to the underground world, as places to be used by persons who wanted to become shaman or to perform magical arts. This gives an impression of the large variability in the use of naturally confined localities which would remain undetected without written sources. Just by excavation alone it is impossible to understand the significance of these sites.

In Greenland caves, rock shelters and boulders are spatially and temporally stable elements of a landscape well known by its human users. The localities are known in their geographical position, as is shown by names for sites, their relation to other sites, their history and their site-specific characteristics. Therefore research in the interior of Central West Greenland let us assume that the most important reason how caves, rock shelters and boulders are used seems to lie in their relationship to other sites and therefore in their position in the cultural landscape. The low number of rock shelter sites in the research area has to be emphasized. Not more than one tenth of all archaeological sites are represented by rock shelters. Maybe regions far away from primary access routes have more rock shelters whereas hunting in areas with fast access did not depend that much on naturally confined sites.

The inland of West Greenland was used more or less continuously to hunt caribou in summer which led to the same travel routes and successive occupation of nearly the same localities by different generations sometimes over centuries. This may show that open-air sites in the inland of Central West Greenland were also fixed localities in time and space – a characteristic which is not an exclusive element of caves and rock shelters.

The pattern of inland use changed due to fluctuations of the caribou population in cycles of approximately 100 years: During a caribou population maximum several groups with many people travelled inland and used large camps for communal hunting. During a caribou population minimum just a few, very mobile hunters penetrate the inland region staying for only a short time at a number of different localities. However, caves and rock shelters may have always been used independently of these changes in settlement and subsistence patterns, each time with the same goal (as resting and sleeping place during travel inland and back as well as on special hunting expeditions) and the same group size and composition (few individual hunters). This interpretation is supported by archaeological evidence: In contrast to open-air sites, where differences in site use resulted in the alteration of structures built during a previous occupation, structures in rock shelters were not changed but just maintained. Therefore the use and function of rock shelter sites remained the same over centuries. As material evidence in open-air sites may reflect changes in settlement and subsistence patterns better than archaeological evidence preserved in rock shelters, the creation of landscape drawn out through time by people who moved in it may be investigated the best in open-air sites.

A comparison between suitable open-air sites and rock shelter sites suggests that there are no differences in behaviour when small numbers of mobile caribou-hunters built and used short-term resting and sleeping places in the research area. This may imply that the specific characteristics of naturally confined localities determine their use less than do the technology, material knowledge, perception of space and symbolic occupation by a particular culture.

Research in Greenland was not done to have an analogy for the Palaeolithic in Europe. The investigation was made to establish a testable correspondence between the living culture of arctic hunter-gatherers and its archaeological consequences. With that archaeologists can expand their knowledge about people which lived at other times and in other parts of the world and therefore prevent Palaeolithic archaeology from taking processes and relations found in our own culture as deriving from human nature.

Bibliography

Anawak, J. 1989. Inuit perceptions of the past. In: *Who needs the past.* Layton, R. (Ed.) London: One World Archaeology 5: 45-50.

Anderson, N.J. and Brodersen, K.P 2001. Determining the date of ice-melt for low Arctic lakes along Søndre Strømfjord, southern West Greenland. *Geology of Greenland Survey Bulletin* 189: 54-58.

Anderson, N.J., Clarke, A., Juhler, R.K., McGowan, S. and Renberg, I. 2000. Coring of laminated lake sediments for pigment and mineral magnetic analyses, Søndre Strømfjord, Southern West Greenland. *Geology of Greenland Survey Bulletin* 186: 83-87.

Anderson, N.J., Fritz, S.C., Gibson, C.E., Hasholt, B. and Leng, M.J. 2002: Lake-catchment interactions with climate in the low Arctic of southern West Greenland. *Geology of Greenland Survey Bulletin* 191: 144-149.

Andreasen, C. 2003: Inuit cultures in Greenland. In: *Mummies in a new millenium.* Lynnerup, N., Andreasen, C. and Berglund, J. (Eds.) Copenhagen: Danish Polar Center Publications 11: 11-16.

Amdrup, G. 1909. *The former Eskimo settlements on the east coast of Greenland.* Copenhagen: Meddelelser om Grønland 28,4: 285-328.

Appelt, M. 1999. David Site. In: *Late Dorset in High Arctic Greenland.* Appelt, M. and Gulløv, H.C. (Eds.) Copenhagen: Danish Polar Center Publication 7: 24-41.

Appelt, M., Gulløv, H.C., Hanna, D., Kapel, H., LeMoine, G. and Møhl, J. 1998. The gateway to Greenland – Appendix 1: archaeology. – In: *Man, culture and environment in ancient Greenland.* Arneborg, J. and Gulløv, H.C. (Eds.) Copenhagen: Danish Polar Center Publication 4: 154-187.

Arsenault, D., Gagnon, L. and Gendron, D. 1998. Investigations archéologique récentes au sud de Kangirsujuaq et sur le site à pétroglyphes de l'île Qajartalik, détroit d'Hudson, Nunavik. *Études/Inuit/Studies* 22: 77-116.

Balme, J. and Beck, W.E. 2002. Starch and charcoal: useful measures of activity areas in archaeological rock shelters. *Journal of Archaeological Science* 29: 157-166.

Barton, C.M. and Clark, G.A. 1993. Cultural and natural formation processes in Late Quaternary cave and rock shelter sites of Western Europa and the Near East. In: *Formation processes in archaeological context.* Goldberg, P., Nash, D.T. and Petraglia, M.D. (Eds.) Madison: Monographs in World Archaeology 17: 33-52.

Barrett, J.C. 1999. Chronologies of landscape. In: *The archaeology and anthropology of landscape.* Ucko, P.J. and Layton, R. (Eds.) London: 21-30.

Bar-Yosef, O. 1993. Site formation processes from a Levantine viewpoint. In: *Formation processes in archaeological context.* Goldberg, P., Nash, D.T. and Petraglia, M.D. (Eds.) Madison: Monographs in World Archaeology 17: 13-32.

Begouën, R., Clottes, J., Giraud, J.-P. and Rouzaud, F. 1989. Les foyers de la caverne d'Enlène (Montesquieu-Avantès, Ariège). In: *Nature et fonction des foyers préhistoriques.* Olive, M. and Taborin Y. (Dir.) Nemours: Mémoire de la Musée Préhistorique de l'Ile de France 2: 165-179.

Clemens Pasda

Begouën, R., Clottes, J., Giraud, J.-P. and R. Rouzaud, F. 1996. Os plantés et peintures rupestres dans la caverne d'Enlène. In: *Pyrénées Préhistoriques – arts et sociétés*. Delporte, H. and Clottes, J. (Dir.) Paris: 283-306.

Bender, B. 1993. Introduction: landscape – meaning and action. In: *Landscape: politics and perspectives*. Bender, B. (Ed.) Oxford: 1-17.

   - 1999. Subverting the Western Gaze: mapping alternative wolds. In: *The archaeology and anthropology of landscape*. Ucko, P.J. and Layton, R. (Eds.) London: 31-45.

   - 2001. Introduction. In: *Contested landscapes: movement, exile and place*. Bender, B. and Winer, M. (Eds.) Oxford: 1-18.

Berglund, J. 2002. Kirkespirsdalen – 'Church Spire Valley'. Nuuk: http://www.natmus.gl./en/maanhi/august/body_august.html.

Bernbeck, R. 1997. *Theorien in der Archäologie*. München.

Berthelsen, C., Mortensen, I.H. and Mortensen, E. 1997. *Kalaallit Nunaat/Grønland Atlas*. Nuuk.

Bielawski, E. 1989. Dual perceptions of the past: archaeology and Inuit culture. In: *Conflicts in the archaeology of living traditions*. Layton, R. (Ed.) London: 228-236.

Binford, L.R. 1978. *Nunamiut Ethnoarchaeology*. New York/London.

Binford, L.R. 1996. Hearth and home: the spatial analysis of ethnographically documented rock shelter occupations as a template for distinguishing between human and hominid use of sheltered space. In: *Middle Palaeolithic and Middle Stone Age settlement systems*. Conard N.J. and Wendorf, F. (Coord.) Forli: Proceedings of the XIIIth Congress U.I.S.P.P.: 229-235.

Birket-Smith, K. 1917. *Foreløbigt bidrag til Kap Farvel-distrikternes kulturhistorie*. København: Meddelelser om Grønland 103.

   - 1924. *Ethnography of the Egedesminde District*. Copenhagen: Meddelelser om Grønland 66.

   - 1948. *Die Eskimos*. Zürich.

Bonsall, C. and Tolan-Smith, C. (Eds.) 1997. *The human use of caves*. Oxford: BAR International Series 667.

Brodersen, K.P. and Anderson, N.J. 2000. Subfossil insect remains (Chironomidae) and lake-water temperature inference in the Sisimiut-Kangerlussuaq region, southern West Greenland. *Geology of Greenland Survey Bulletin* 186: 78-82.

Brodersen, K.P., Lindegaard, C. and N.J. Johnson, N.J. 2001. Holocene temperature and environmental reconstruction from lake sediments in the Søndre Strømfjord region, southern West Greenland. *Geology of Greenland Survey Bulletin* 189: 59-64.

Brochier, J.E., Villa, P. and Giacomarra, M. 1992. Shepherds and sediments: Geo-ethnoarchaeology of pastoral sites. *Journal of Anthropological Archaeology* 11: 47-102.

Burch Jr., E.S. 1975. Inter-regional transportation in traditional Northwest Alaska. *Anthropological Papers of the University of Alaska* 17-2: 1-12.

Bøcher, J., Feilberg, J., Folving, S., Hansen, P., Hasholt, B., Jacobsen, N.K., Kristensen, K., Krogh, K., Meldgaard, J., Petersen, H.C. and Sørgaard, H. 1980. *Holsteinsborg – Sisimiut kommune. Natur- og kulturforhold.* Udvalget vedrørende Fredningslov for Grønland. Ministeriet for Grønland.

Bøcher, T.W. 1949. *Climate, soil, and lakes in continental West Greenland in relation to plant life.* Copenhagen: Meddelelser om Grønland 147, 2.

- 1963. *Phytogeography of Middle West Greenland.* Copenhagen: Meddelelser om Grønland 148, 3.

Cinq-Mars, I. 1979. Bluefish Cave 1: A late Pleistocene Eastern Beringia cave deposit in the Northern Yukon. *Canadian Journal of Archaeology* 3: 1-32.

Clifford, J. 1988. On ethnographic authority. In: *The predicament of culture.* Clifford, J. (Ed.) Cambridge: 21-54.

Clifford, J. and Marcus, G.E. (Eds.) 1986. *Writing culture.* Berkeley.

Clottes, J. 1993. Le contexte archéologique externe – le context archéologique interne – Ichnologie. In: *L'art paléolithique.* Paris : 27-35; 49-58; 59-66.

Cosgrove, D. 1984. *Social formation and symbolic landscape.* London.

Cruikshank, J. 2001. Glaciers and climate: perspectives from oral tradition. *Arctic* 54: 377-393.

Cuyler, C., Rosing, M., Linnell, J.D.C., Loison, A., Ingerslev, T. and Landa, A. 2002. Status of the Kangerlussuaq-Sisimiut caribou population (*Rangifer tarandus groenlandicus*) in 2000, West Greenland. *Greenland Institute of Natural Resources – Technical Report 42.* Nuuk.

Dahl, J. 2000. *Saqqaq – An Inuit hunting community in the modern world.* Toronto.

Daniel, U. 2002. *Kompendium Kulturgeschichte.* Frankfurt/Main.

Danielsen, J., Rasmussen, K. and Rosendahl, P. 1967: *Kâgssagssuk – The legend of the orphan boy.* Lyngby.

David, N. and Kramer, C. 2001. *Ethnoarchaeology in action.* Cambridge.

Dawes, P.R., Elander, M. and Ericson, M. 1986. The wolf (Canis lupus) in Greenland: a historical review and present status. *Arctic* 39: 119-132.

Degerbøl, M. 1936. *The former Eskimo habitation in the Kangerdlugssuak District, East Greenland.* Copenhagen: Meddelelser om Grønland 104, 10.

Doubleday, N. 1999. Arctic worlds and the geography of imagination. In: *Nature and identity in cross-cultural perspective.* Buttimer, A. and Wallin, L. (Eds.) Dordrecht: 189-198.

Everett, K.R. 1967. *Mass-wasting in the Tasersiaq area, West Greenland.* Copenhagen: Meddelelser om Grønland 165, 5.

Eriksen, B.V. 1991. *Change and continuity in a prehistoric hunter-gatherer society: a study of cultural adaptation in late glacial-early postglacial southwestern Germany.* Tübingen.

Escher, A., Sørensen, K. and Zeck, H.P. 1976. Nagssugtoqidian mobile belt in West Greenland. In: *Geology of Greenland.* Escher, A. and Watt, W.S. (Eds.) Copenhagen: 77-95.

Farrand, W.R. 1985. Rock shelter and cave sediments. In: *Archaeological sediments in context.* Stein, J.K. and Farrand, W.R. (Eds.) Orono: Peopling of the Americas 1: 21-39.

- 1993. Discontinuity in the stratigraphic record: snapshots from Franchthi Cave. In: *Formation processes in archaeological context.* Goldberg, P., Nash, D.T. and Petraglia, M.D. (Eds.) Madison: Monographs in World Archaeology 17: 85-96.

- 2001. Sediments and stratigraphy in rock shelters and caves: A personal perspectives on principles and pragmatics. *Geoarchaeology* 16: 537-557.

Fernández-Jalvo, V. and Andrews, P. 2000. The taphonomy of Pleistocene caves, with particular reference to Gibraltar. *Neanderthals on the edge.* Stringer, C.B., Barton, R.N.E. and Finlayson, J.L. (Eds.) Oxford: 171-182.

Ferguson, M.A.D. and Messier, F. 1997. Collection and analysis of traditional ecological knowledge about a population of arctic tundra caribou. *Arctic* 50: 17-28.

Ferguson, M.A.D., Williamson, R.G. and Messier, F. 1998. Inuit knowledge of long-term changes in a population of arctic tundra caribou. *Arctic* 51: 201-219.

Fischer-Møller, K. 1938. *Skeletons from ancient Greenland graves.* Copenhagen: Meddelelser om Grønland 119,4.

Fortescue, M. 1988. *Eskimo orientation systems.* Copenhagen: Meddelelser om Gønland – Man & Society 11.

Gabriel, M., Grønnow, B., Odgaard, U., Pasda, C. and Pasda, K. 2002. Bosættelsmønstre i det Centrale Vestgrønland – Rapport om undersøgelserne i Angujaartorfiup Nunaa, Maniitsoq Kommune, sommeren 2001. *SILA-Feltrapport* 4. Nationalmuseet København.

Galanidou, N. 1997. *'Home is where the hearth is' - The spatial organisation of the Upper Palaeolithic rock shelter occupation at Klithi and Kastritsa in Northwest Greece.* Oxford: BAR International Series 687.

Galanidou, N. 1998. Uses of ethnography in modelling Palaeolithic settlement: the past, the present and the future. *Préhistoire Européenne* 13: 195-204.

Galanidou, N. 2000. Patterns in caves: foragers, horticulturalists, and the use of space. *Journal of Anthropological Archaeology* 19: 243-275.

Gamble, C. 1991. An introduction to the living spaces of mobile peoples. In: *Ethnoarchaeological approaches to mobile campsites.* Gamble, C.S. and Boismier, W.A. (Eds.) Ann Arbor: International Monographs in Prehisory – Ethnoarchaeological Series 1: 1-23.

Gamble, C. 2001. *Archaeology – The basics.* London.

Garcia, M.A. and Rouzaud, F. 2001. Scène de chasse en Ariège. *Bulletin de la Soçiété Prehistorique Ariège-Pyrénées* 54 : 79-82.

Geertz, C. 1988. *Works and lives – The anthropologist as author.* Stanford.

Georgina, D.M. 2001. The small mammals of Lime Hills Cave I, Alaska. In: *People and wildlife in northern North America – Essays in honour of R. Dale Guthrie.* Gerlach, S.C. and Murray, M.S. (Eds.) Oxford: BAR Interntional Series 944: 25-31.

Giesecke, K.L. 1910. *Bericht einer mineralogischen Reise in Grönland.* Copenhagen: Meddelelser om Grønland 35.

Gilberg, R. 1984. Polar Eskimo. In: *Handbook of North American Indians Vol. 5 – Arctic.* Damas, D. (Ed.) Washington: 577-594.

Glob, P.V. 1935. *Eskimo settlements in Kempe Fjord and King Oscar Fjord.* Copenhagen: Meddelelser om Grønland 102,2.

Golledge, R.G. 2003. Human wayfinding and cognitive maps. In: *Colonization of unfamiliar landscapes.* Rockman, M. and Steele, J. (Eds.) London: 25-43.

Gosden, C. 1999. *Anthropology & Archaeology – A changing relationship.* London.

  - 2001. Postcolonial archaeology – Issues of culture, identity, and knowledge. In: *Archaeological theory today.* Hodder, I. (Ed.) Cambridge: 241-261.

Gosden, C. and Head, L. 1994. Landscape – a usefully ambigeous concept. *Archaeology of Oceania* 29: 113-116.

Gripp, K. 1941/42. Grönländische Rentierjäger. *Offa* 6/7: 40-51.

Grote, K. 1990. Das Buntsandsteinabri Bettenroder Berg IX im Rheinhäuser Wald bei Göttingen – Paläolithikum und Mesolithikum. *Archäologisches Korrespondenzblatt* 20: 137-147.

Grønnow, B. 1986. Recent archaeological investigations of West Greenland caribou hunting. *Arctic Anthropology* 23: 57-80.

  - 1999: Qallunatalik/Polaris Site. In: *Late Dorset in High Arctic Greenland.* Appelt, M. and Gulløv, H.C. (Eds.) Copenhagen: Danish Polar Center Publication 7: 42-62.

Grønnow, B. and Jensen, J.F. 2003. *The northernmost ruins of the globe.* Copenhagen: Monogrophs of Greenland – Man & Society 29.

Grønnow, B., Meldgaard, M. and Nielsen, J.B. 1983. *Aasivissuit – The great summer camp.* Copenhagen: Meddelelser om Grønland - Man & Society 5.

Grummesgaard-Nielsen, S. 1997. Thulekulturens grave. *Tidsskriftet Grønland* 5-7: 198-227.

Guldager, O., Hansen, S.S. and Gleie, E. 2002. *Medieval farmsteads in Greenland – The Brattahlid region 1999-2000.* Copenhagen: Danish Polar Center Publication 9.

Gulløv, H.C. 1983. *Nuup kommuneani qangarnitsanik eqqaassutit inuit-kulturip nunaqarfi – Fortidsminder i Nuuk kommune – inuit-kulturens bopladser.* Nuuk.

  - 1997. *From Middle Ages to Colonial times – Archaeological and ethnohistorical studies of the Thule culture in South West Greenland 1300-1800 AD.* Copenhagen: Meddelelser om Grønland - Man & Society 23.

  - 2000. Østgrønlandsk kartografi og xylografi. In: *Topografisk Atlas Grønland.* København: 170-171.

Hahn, J. 1984. Spatial organisation and occupation of the Helga-Abri, near Schelklingen, Swabian Jura. In: *Jungpaläolithische Siedlungsstrukturen in Europa.* Berke, H., Hahn, J. and Kind, C.-J. (Eds.) Tübingen: Urgeschichtliche Materialhefte 6: 79-86.

Clemens Pasda

- 1986. *Kraft und Aggression*. Tübingen.

- 1989/90. Von Höhlenmenschen und Höhlenbären. Zur urgeschichtlichen Erforschung von Höhlen. *Karst und Höhle*: 177-183.

- 1993. Aurignacian art in Central Europe. In: *Before Lascaux*. Knecht, H. (Ed.) Boca Raton: 229-241.

Hallendy, N. 1994. Inuksuit – Semalithic figures constructed by Inuit in the Canadian Arctic. In: *Threads of Arctic Prehistory – Papers in honour of William E. Taylor Jr.* Morrison, D. and Pilon J.-L. (Eds.) Ottawa: Canadian Museum of Civilization, Mercury Series, Archaeological Survey of Canada Paper 149: 385-408.

- 2000. *Inuksuit – Silent messengers of the Arctic*. Seattle.

Hansen, J.P. and Gulløv, H.C. (Eds.) 1989. *The mummies from Qilakitsoq – Eskimos in the 15th century*. Copenhagen: Meddelelser om Grønland – Man & Society 12.

Hansen, J.P., Meldgaard, J. and Nordqvist, J. 1991. *The Greenland mummies*. London.

Hansen, K. 1970. *Geological and geographical investigations in Kong Frederiks IX's Land*. Copenhagen: Meddelelser om Grønland 188,4.

Hansen, K.G. and Larsen, N. 2002. *Interviews with Geerteeraq Dahl (from Itilleq), Laarseeraq „Assa" Enoksen (from Sarfannguaq), Seth Olesen (from Ikerasaarsuk) and Ulrik Lennert (from Sarfannguaq)*. Unpublished manuscript, recorded by N. Larsen in 2001, english translation by K.G. Hansen. Sisimiut: 10 pp.

Hansen, S. 1893. *Bidrag til Vestgrønlændernes Anthropologi*. København: Meddelelser om Grønland 7.

Hansen, T. et al. 1978. *Kornerups Grønland*. Copenhagen.

Hearne, S. 1981. *Abenteuer im arktischen Kanada – Die Suche nach der Nordwest-Passage 1769-1772*. Darmstadt.

Hehmsoth-LeMouël, M. 1999. The presence of intact, complete artifacts in archaeological sites: indicators of a rupture in the way of life? In: *Ethno-analogy and the reconstruction of prehistoric artefact use and production*. Owen, L.R. and Porr, M. (Eds.) Tübingen: Urgeschichtliche Materialhefte 14: 75-90.

Hjarnø, J. 1974. *Eskimo graves from Upernavik District – Archaeological and anthropological investigations of late heathen graves in Upernavik District*. Copenhagen: Meddelelser om Grønland 202,1: 9-35.

Holm, G. 1914. *Ethnological sketch of the Angmassalik Eskimo*. Copenhagen: Meddelelser om Grønland 39,1.

Holtved, E. 1944. *Archaeological investigations in the Thule District I*. Copenhagen: Meddelelser om Grønland 141,1.

- 1967. *Contributions to Polar Eskimo ethnography*. Copenhagen: Meddelelser om Grønland 182,2.

Ingold, T. 2000. *The perception of the environment*. London/New York.

Israel, H. 1969. Kulturwandel grönländischer Eskimo im 18. Jahrhundert. *Abhandlungen und Berichte des Staatlichen Museums für Völkerkunde Dresden* 29. Berlin.

Jensen, J.F. 1996. Paleo-Eskimo sites in Skjoldungen District, South East Greenland. In: *The Paleo-Eskimo-cultures of Greenland – New perspectives in Greenlandic archaeology.* Grønnow (Ed.) Copenhagen: Danish Polar Center Publication 1: 143-159.

McI. Johnson, D. 1933. *Observations on the Eskimo remains on the east coast of Greenland between 72° and 75° north latitude.* Copenhagen: Meddelelser om Grønland 92,6.

Jørgensen, J.B. 1989. Anthropology of the Qilakitsoq Eskimos. In: *The mummies from Qilakitsoq – Eskimos in the 15th century.* Hansen, J.P. and Gulløv, H.C. (Eds.) Copenhagen: Meddelesler om Grønland – Man & Society 12: 56-57.

Kapel, H. 1996. Angujaartorfik – a Paleo-Eskimo caribou hunting camp. In: *The Paleo-Eskimo-cultures of Greenland – New perspectives in Greenlandic archaeology.* Grønnow, B. (Ed.) Copenhagen: Danish Polar Center Publication 1: 119-128.

Kelly, R.L. 1995. *The foraging spectrum.* Washington.

  - 2003. Colonization of new land by hunter-gatherers. In: *Colonization of unfamiliar landscapes.* Rockman, M. and Steele, J. (Eds.) London: 44-58.

Klein, D.R. 1994. Wilderness – a concept alien to arctic cultures. *Informations North* 20: 1-6.

Kleivan, H. 1984. Greenland Eskimo – introduction. In: *Handbook of North American Indians Vol. 5 – Arctic.* Damas, D. (Ed.) Washington: 522-527.

Knapp, A.B. and Ashmore, W. 1999. Archaeological landscapes: construced, conceptualized. Ideational. In: *Archaeologies of landscape.* Ashmore, W. and Knapp, A.B. (Eds.) Oxford: 1-30.

Knuth, E. 1981. Greenland news from between 81° and 83° north. *Folk* 23: 91-111.

Koch, A. and Felbo, M. 1994. Thulekulturens grave. *Tusaat – Forskning i Grønland* 1994/1-2: 35-45.

Kötter, R. 2001. Zur methodologischen Struktur des Aktualismusprinzips. *Zeitschrift der deutschen geologischen Gesellschaft* 152: 129-141.

Kramer, F.E. 1996. The Paleo-Eskimo cultures in Sisimiut District, West Greenland. In: *The Paleo-Eskimo-cultures of Greenland – New perspectives in Greenlandic archaeology.* Grønnow, B. (Ed.) Copenhagen: Danish Polar Center Publication 1: 39-63.

Lauriol, B., Prévost, C., Deschamps, E., Cinq-Mars, J. and Labrecque, S. 2001. Faunal and archaeological remains as evidence of climate change in freezing caverns, Yukon Territory, Canada. *Arctic* 54: 135-147.

Larsen, H. 1934: *Dødemansbugten – an Eskimo settlement on Clavering Island.* Copenhagen: Meddelelser om Grønland 102,1.

  - 1938. *Archaeological investigations on Knud Rasumussens Land.* Copenhagen: Meddelelser om Grønland 119,8.

  - 1968. *Trail Creek: Final report on the excavations of two caves on Seward Peninsula, Alaska.* Copenhagen.

Layton, R. and Ucko, P.J. 1999. Introduction: Gazing on the landscape and encountering the environment. In: *The archaeology and anthropology of landscape*. Ucko, P.J. and Layton, R. (Eds.) London: 1-20.

Lee, M. and Reinhardt, G.A. 2003. *Eskimo architecture*. Fairbanks.

LeMouël, J.-F. 1978. „*Ceux des mouttes"* – *Les Eskimo naujâmiut, Groënland-Ouest*. Paris: Documents d´écologie humaine. Mémoire de l´Institute d´Ethnolologie 26.

Leser, H. 1997. *Wörterbuch Allgemeine Geographie*. München.

Lidegaard, M. 1986. Profeterne i Evighedsfjorden. *Tidskriftet Grønland*: 177-244.

Lorblanchet, M. 1999. De l´art des grottes à l´art de plein air au Paléolithique. In: *L´art paléolitique à l´air libre*. Sacchi, D. (Ed.) Tautavel : 97-112.

Lowe, J.J. and Walker, MJ.C. 1999. *Reconstructing quaternary environments*. Harlow (2nd. edition).

Lüning, J. 1997. Landschaftsarchäologie in Deutschland – Ein Programm. *Archäologisches Nachrichtenblatt* 2: 277-285.

Lyman, R.L., Savelle, J.M. and Whitridge, P. 1992. Derivation and application of a meat utility index for phocid seals. *Journal of Archaeological Science* 19: 531-555.

Lynnerup, N. 2003. The Greenland mummies. In: *Mummies in a new millenium*. Lynnerup, N., Andreasen, C. and Berglund, J. (Eds.) Copenhagen: Danish Polar Center Publications 11: 17-19.

MacDonald, J. 1998. *The arctic sky – Inuit astronomy, star lore and legend*. Toronto.

Marcus, G.E. and Fischer, M.M.J. (Eds.) 1986. *Anthropology as culture critique*. Chicago.

Mathiassen, Th. 1928. Material culture of the Iglulik Eskimos. Copenhagen: *Report of the Fifth Thule Expedition 1921-24:* Vol. VI, 1.

- 1930. *Inugsuk, a mediaeval Eskimo settlement in Upernavik District, West Greenland.* Copenhagen: Meddelelser om Grønland 77,4: 145-338.

- 1931. *Ancient Eskimo settlements in the Kangâmiut area.* Copenhagen: Meddelelser om Grønland 91,1.

- 1933: *Prehistory of the Amagssalik Eskimos.* Copenhagen: Meddelelser om Grønland 92,4.

- 1934. *Contributions to the archaeology of Disko Bay.* Copenhagen: Meddelelser om Grønland 93,2.

- 1936a. *The former Eskimo settlement on Frederiks VI´s coast.* Copenhagen: Meddelelser om Grønland 109,2.

- 1936b. *The Eskimo archaeology of Julianehaab District.* Copenhagen: Meddelelser om Grønland 118,1.

Maxwell, M.S. 1985. *Prehistory of the Eastern Arctic*. Orlando.

Mayer, C., Bøggild, C.E., Podlech, S., Olesen, O.B., Ahlstrøm, A.P. and Krabill, W. 2002. Glaciological investigations on ice-sheet response in South Greenland. *Geology of Greenland Survey Bulletin* 191: 150-156.

Meldgaard, J. 1953. Fra en grønlandsk mumiehule. *Nationalmuseets Arbejdsmark*: 14-20.

Meldgaard, J., Rosing, J. and Hansen, K. 1971. *Grønlandske fangere fortæller*. København.

Meldgaard, M. 1983. Resource fluctuations and human subsistence – a zoo-archaeological and ethnographical investigation of a West Greenland caribou hunting camp. In: *Animals and archaeology 1 – Hunters and their prey*. Clutton-Brock/Grigson, C. (Eds.) Oxford: BAR International Series 163: 259-272.

- 1986. *The Greenland caribou – zoogeography, taxonomy, and population daynamics*. Copenhagen: Meddelelser om Grønland - Bioscience. 20.

- 1997. Sisikasiit: the place with the fox holes. In: *Fifty years of arctic research*. Gilberg, R. and Gulløv, H.C. (Eds.) Copenhagen: Publications of the National Museum. Ethnographical Serie 18: 215-220.

Moser, J. 1999. Recent cave dwellings in Southeast Asia: home, domiciles or refuges? Explanation and interpretation of prehistoric archaeological structures. In: *Ethno-analogy and the reconstruction of prehistoric artefact use and production*. Owen, L.R. and Porr, M. (Eds.) Tübingen: Urgeschichtliche Materialhefte 14: 275-284.

Müller-Beck, H. 1983. Urgeschichte in Baden-Württemberg – Eine Einführung. In: *Urgeschichte in Baden-Württemberg*. Müller-Beck, H. (Hrsg.) Stuttgart: 13-31.

Müller-Beck, H. 1986. Strukturplanung Institut für Urgeschichte. *Mitteilungsblatt Archaeologica Venatoria* 10/11: 44-68.

Münzel, S. 2002. Cave bear hunting on the Swabian Alb (Germany), 30.000 years ago. In: Cave-Bear-Researches/Höhlen-Bären-Forschungen. Rosendahl, W., Morgan, M. and López Correa, M. (Eds.) *Abhandlungen zur Karst- und Höhlenkunde* 34: 36-39.

Münzel, S., Morel, Ph. and Hahn, J. 1994. Jungpleistozäne Tierreste aus der Geißenklösterle-Höhle bei Blaubeuren. *Fundberichte aus Baden-Württemberg* 19/1: 63-93.

Münzel, S., Langguth, K., Conard, N.J. and Uerpmann, H.-P. 2001. Höhlenbärenjagd auf der Schwäbischen Alb vor 30.000 Jahren. *Archäologisches Korrespondenzblatt* 31: 317-328.

Muir, R. 1999. *Approaches to landscape*. London.

Møbjerg, T. 1998. The Saqqaq culture in the Sisimiut District municipality elucidated by two sites – Nipisat and Asummiut. In: *Man, culture and environment in ancient Greenland*. Arneborg, J. and Gulløv, H.C. (Eds.) Copenhagen: Danish Polar Center Publication 4: 98-118.

Møbjerg, T. and Caning, K. 1986. Sermermiut in the middle of the nineteenth century. *Arctic Anthropology* 23: 177-198.

Møbjerg, T. and Robert-Lamblin, J. 1989. The settlement at Ikaasap Ittiva, East Greenland. *Acta Archaeologica* 60: 229-262.

Nansen, F. 1991. *Eskimoleben*. Berlin.

Nellemann, G. 1969/70. Caribou hunting in West Greenland. *Folk* 11-12: 133-153.

Nicholson, A. and Cane, R. 1991. Desert camps: analysis of Australian Aboriginal proto-historic campsites. In: *Ethnoarchaeological approaches to mobile campsites*. Gamble, C.S. and Boismier, W.A. (Eds.) Ann Arbor: International Mongraphs in Prehistory: 355-370.

Nuttall, M. 2000. Becoming a hunter in Greenland. *Études/Inuit/Studies* 24: 33-45.

Nyegaard, G. 1995. Qaqortup Katersugaasivia/Julianehåb Museum. *Archaeological field work in the Northwest Territories in 1994, and in Greenland in 1993 and 1994.* Prince of Wales, Northern Heritage Center – Archaeological Report 16: 101-103.

O´Connell, J.F. 1995. Ethnoarchaeology needs a general theory of behaviour. *Journal of Archaeological Research* 3: 205-255.

Odgaard, U., Grønnow, B., Gabriel, M., Pasda, C., Pasda, K. and Damm, C. 2003. Bosættelsmønstre i det Centrale Vestgrønland – Rapport om undersøgelserne i Angujaartorfiup Nunaa, Maniitsoq Kommune, sommeren 2002. Nationalmuseet København: *SILA-Feltrapport 12.*

Olesen, C.R. 1991. The musk ox in Angujaartorfiup Nunaa. In: *Conservation of nature in Greenland.* Egede, I. (Ed.) Nuuk: 110-120.

Olesen, C.R., Thing, H. and Aastrup, P. 1994. Growth of wild muskoxen under two nutritional regions in Greenland. *Rangifer* 14/1: 3-10.

Ostermann, H. 1921. Christianshaab District. In: *Grønland i tohundredaaret for Hans Egedes landning I.* København: Meddelelser om Grønland 110: 90-150.

Ostermann, H. 1938. *Knud Rasmussen´s posthumous notes on the life and doings of the East Greenlanders in olden times.* Copenhagen: Meddelelser om Grønland 109,1.

Owens, D.A. and Hayden, B. 1997. Prehistoric rites of passage: a comparative study of transegalitarian hunter-gatherers. *Journal of Anthropological Archaeology* 16: 121-161.

Pasda, C. 1998. *Wildbeuter im archäologischen Kontext.* Bad Bellingen.

Pasda, C. and K. 1999. The use of caves and rock shelters by historic Inuit in West Greenland. *Unpublished field report.* University of Erlangen-Nuremberg.

Pasda, C. and K. 2000. The use of caves and rock shelters by historic Inuit in West Greenland. *Unpublished field report.* University of Erlangen-Nuremberg.

Pasda, C. 2001. Faunalturbation unter Felsüberhängen – Beispiele für Störungen durch Tiere der arktischen Tundra. *Ethnographisch-Archäologische Zeitschrift* 42: 321-333.

Pasda, C. 2002. Die urgeschichtliche Fundlandschaft: Zeugnis einer Kulturlandschaft – Ergebnisse der Surveys im Inland von Westgrönland 1999-2000. *Ethnographisch- Archäologische Zeitschrift* 43: 323-376.

Pasda, C. 2003. Übernachten ohne Dach unter arktischen Klimabedingungen - Das hunters´ bed in Westgrönland. *Quartär* 53/54: in print.

Pasda, K. 2001. Zur Taphonomie von Rentieren (Rangifer tarandus groenlandicus) in der Tundra Westgrönlands. *Quartär* 51/52: 173-194.

Pasternak, S. 1999. *Oqaluttuartoq Jens Rosing - Fortælleren Jens Rosing – Jens Rosing the storyteller.* Nuuk.

Pedersen, A. 1936. *Der grönländische Moschusochse.* Kopenhagen: Meddelelser om Grønland 93,7.

Pedersen, S.A.S., Larsen, L.M., Dahl-Larsen, T., Jepsen, H.F., Pedersen, G.K., Nielsen, T., Pedersen, A.K., v. Platen-Hallermund, F. and Wenig, W. 2002. Tsunami-generating rock-fall and landslide on the south coast of Nuussuaq, central West Greenland. *Geology of Greenland Survey Bulletin* 191: 73-83.

Perrin, T., Sordoillet, D. and Voruz, J.L. 2002. L´habitat en grotte au Néolithique: vers une estimation de l´intensité des occupations. *L´Anthropologie* 106: 423-433.

Petersen, H.C. 1986a. Recording the utilization of land and sea resources in Greenland. *Arctic Anthropology* 23, 1-2: 259-269.

Petersen, H.C. 1986b. *Skinboats of Greenland.* Ships and boats of the North 1. Roskilde.

Petersen, H.C. 1997. *Den store kajakbog.* København.

Petersen, M. 2002. „40 or 400 times". Nuuk: http://www.natmus.gl./en/maanhi/april/ body_april.html.

Petersen, R. 1964. The Greenland Tupilak. *Folk* 6: 73-101.

Petersen, R. 1966/67. Burial-forms and death cult among the Eskimos. *Folk* 8-9: 259-280.

Petersen, R. 1973. On the variations of settlement pattern and hunting conditions in three districts of Greenland. In: *Circumpolar problems.* Berg, R. (Ed.) Oxford: 153-161.

Petersen, R. 2003. *Settlement, kinship and hunting grounds in traditional Greenland.* Copenhagen: Monographs on Greenland – Man & Society 27.

Pind, J., Grønnow, B., Ipsen, J., Odgaard, U. and Schilling, H. 1991. *Aasivissuit – Bopladser og rensdyrjagt i det vestgrønlandske indland.* Københavns Universitet.

Plumet, P. 1985. Cairns-balises et mégalithes de l´Ungava. *Études/Inuit/Studies* 9: 61-87.

Porsild, M.P. 1920. On Eskimo stone rows in Greenland formerly supposed to be of Norse origin. *The Geographical Review* 10: 297-309.

Pousaz, N. et al. 1991. *L´abri-sous-roche mésolithique des Gripons à Saint-Ursanne (JU/Suisse).* Porrentruy: Cahier d´archéologie jurassienne 2.

Rink, H. 1875. *Tales and traditions of the Eskimo.* Edinburgh/London (reprint 1997).

Rink, H. 1877. Danish Greenland – Its people and products. London (reprint 1974).

Robbe, P. 1977. Orientation et réperage chez les Tileqilamiut. *Études/Inuit/Studies* 1: 73-83.

Robert-Lamblin, J. 1997. Death in traditional East Greenland: age, causes, and rituals. A contribution from anthropology to archaeology. In: *Fifty years of arctic research.* Gilberg, R. and Gulløv, H.C. (Eds.) Copenhagen: Publication of the National Museum – Ethnographical Series 18: 261-268.

Rockman, M. 2003. Knowledge and learning in the archaeology of colonization. In: *Colonization of unfamiliar landscapes.* Rockman, M. and Steele, J. (Eds.) London: 3-24.

Rosing, J. 1988. Rensdyrjægere i Itinnera. In: *Palæoeskimoisk forskning i Grønland*. Møbjerg, T., Grønnow, B. and Schultz-Lorentzen, H. (Red.) Aarhus: 69-79.

Rott, H. and Obleitner, F. 1992. The energy balance of a dry tundra in West Greenland. *Arctic and Alpine Research* 24: 352-362.

Rowley, S. 1985. Population movements in the Canadian Arctic. *Études/Inuit/Studies* 9: 3-21.

Sandell, H.T. and Sandell, B. 1991. *Archaeology and environment in the Scresby Sund fjord – Ethnoarchaeological investigations of the last Thule culture of Northeast Greenland*. Copenhagen: Meddelelser om Grønland – Man & Society 15.

Sattler, R.A. 1997. Large mammals in Lower Rampart Cave 1, Alaska: interspecific utilization of an Eastern Beringian cave. *Geoarchaeology* 12: 657-688.

Sattler, R.A., Vinson, D.M. and Gillispie, T.E. 2001.Calibrated radiocarbon ages and taphonomic factors in Beringian cave faunas at the end of the Pleistocene. In: *People and wildlife in northern North America – Essays in honour of R. Dale Guthrie*. Gerlach, S.C. and Murray, M.S. (Eds.) Oxford: BAR International Series 944: 112-133.

Schade, C.C.J. 2000. *Landschaftsarchäologie – Eine inhaltliche Begriffsbestimmung*. Bonn: Universitätsforschungen zur Prähistorischen Archäologie 60.

Schama, S. 1995. *Landscape and memory*. New York.

Schilling, H. 1996. Paleo-Eskimo utilization of West Greenland inland areas. In: *The Paleo-Eskimocultures of Greenland – New perspectives in Greenlandic archaeology*. B. Grønnow (Ed.) Copenhagen: Danish Polar Center Publication: 111-118.

Schledermann, P. 1990. *Crossroads to Greenland*. Calgary: Komatik Series 2.

Scholz, H. 1991. Ein Vorstoß des Inlandeises in Westgrönland – Dokumentation des vorrückenden Eisrandes bei Søndre Strømfjord. *Eiszeitalter und Gegenwart* 41: 19-131.

Secher, K., Bøcher, J., Grønnow, B., Holt, S., Petersen, H.C. and Thing, H. 1987. *Arnangarnup Qoorua – Paradisdal i tusinder af år*. Pilersuiffik.

Spikins, P. 2000. Ethno-facts or ethno-fiction? Searching for the structure of settlement patterns. In: *Mesolithic lifeways: current research from Britain and Ireland*. R. Young (Ed.) Leicester: Leicester Archaeology Monographs 7: 105-118.

Spink, J. and Moodie, D.W. 1972. *Eskimo maps from the Canadian Eastern Arctic*. Toronto: Cartographica Monograph 5.

Sommer, U. 1991. *Zur Entstehung archäologischer Fundvergesellschaftungen – Versuch einer archäologischen Taphonomie*. Bonn: Universitätsforschungen zur Prähistorischen Archäologie 6: 51-174.

Sonne, B. 1982. The ideology and practice of blood feuds in East and West Greenland. – *Études/Inuit/Studies* 6: 21-50.

Stahl, A.B. 1993. Concepts of time and approaches to analogical reasoning in historical perspective. *American Antiquity* 58: 235-260.

Steensby, H.P. 1910. *Contributions to the Ethnology and Anthropogeography of the Polar Eskimo.* Copenhagen: Meddelelser om Grønland 34,7.

Stewart, P.J. and Strathern, A. 2003. Introduction. In: *Landscape, memory and history.* Stewart, P.J. and Strathern, A. (Eds.) London: 1-15.

Stoczkowski, W. 2002. *Explaining human origins.* Cambridge.

Straus, L.G. 1973. Caves: a palaeoanthropological resource. *World Archaeology* 10/3: 331-339.

Straus, L.G. 1990. Underground archaeology: perspectives on caves and rock shelters. *Archaeological Method and Theory* 2: 255-304.

Straus, L.G. 1993. Hidden assets and liabilities: exploring archaeology from the earth. In: *Formation processes in archaeological context.* Goldberg, P., Nash, D.T. and Petraglia, M.D. (Eds.) Madison: Monograph in World Archaeology 17: 1-10.

Straus, L.G. 1997. Convenient cavities: some human uses of caves and rock shelters. In: *The human use of caves.* C. Bonsall/C. Tolan-Smith (Eds.) Oxford: BAR International Seris 667: 1-8.

Sørensen, T. and Lynnerup, N. 2003. The mummies from Pisissarfik. In: *Mummies in a new millenium.* Lynnerup, N., Andreasen, C. and Berglund, J. (Eds.) Copenhagen: Danish Polar Center Publications 11: 19-20.

Thalbitzer, W. 1914. *Ethnographical collections from East Greenland.* Copenhagen: Meddelelser om Grønland 39,7: 321-755.

Theunissen, R., Balme, J. and Beck, W. 1998. Headroom and human trampling: cave ceiling height determines the spatial patterning of stone artefacts at Petzkes Cave, northern New South Wales. *Antiquity* 72: 80-89.

Thisted, K. 1997. *Jens Kreutzmann – Fortællinger & akvareller.* Nuuk.

- 1999. *'Således skriver jeg, Aron'- Samlede fortællinger & illustrationer af Aron fra Kangeq.* Nuuk.

Thomas, J. 2001. Archaeologies of place and landscape. In: *Archaeological theory today.* I. Hodder (Ed.) Cambridge: 165-186.

Thostrup, C.H. 1917. *Ethnographic description of the Eskimo settlements and stone remains in North-East Greenland.* Copenhagen: Meddelelser om Grønland 64,4.

Trebitsch, R. 1910. *Bei den Eskimos in Westgrönland – Ergebnisse einer Sommerreise im Jahre 1906.* Berlin.

Trimmel, H. 1968. *Höhlenkunde.* Braunschweig.

Usher, P.J. 2000. Traditional ecological knowledge in enronmental assessment and management. *Arctic* 53: 183-193.

Utrilla, P., Mazo, C. and Domingo, R. 2003. Les structures de l'occupation magdalénienne de la grotte d'Abauntz (Navarre, Espagne). In: *Perceived landscapes and built environments.* Vasil'ev, S.A., Soffer, O. and Kozlowski, J. (Eds.) Oxford: BAR International Series 1122: 25-37.

Clemens Pasda

Vibe, C. 1967. *Arctic animals in relation to climate fluctuations*. Copenhagen: Meddelelser om Grønland 170,15.

Walthall, J.A. 1998. Rock shelters and hunter-gatherer adaptation to the Pleistocene/Holocene boundary. *American Antiquity* 63: 223-238.

Willemse, N. 2000. *Arctic natural archives – Lake and eolian sedimentary records from West Greenland*. Utrecht.

Zvelebil, M. and Fewster, K.J. 2001. Pictures at an exhibition: Ethnoarchaeology and hunter-gatherers. In: *Ethnoarchaeology and hunter-gatherers: pictures at an exhibition*. Zvelebil, M. and Fewster, K.J. (Eds.) Oxford: BAR International Series 955: 143-157.

Zedeño, M.N. and Stoffle, R.W. 2003. Tracking the role of pathways in the evolution of a human landscape. In: *Colonization of unfamiliar landscapes*. Rockman, M. and Steele, J. (Eds.) London: 59-79.

Address of author:

Clemens Pasda
Professur für Urgeschichte
Bereich für Ur- und Frühgeschichte
Friedrich Schiller-Universität Jena
Löbdergraben 24a
D – 07743 Jena
Germany

clemens.pasda@uni-jena.de

www.ingramcontent.com/pod-product-compliance
Lightning Source LLC
Chambersburg PA
CBHW051306270326

41926CB00030B/4749